Whine & Crackers

Musings of a High School Principal

Joe Pelanconi

PWJ Publishing
Tehama, California

ACKNOWLEDGMENTS

I wish to thank the following members of my research team for their invaluable help in making this book possible:

- ❖ Every high school kid I ever met
- ❖ My family, who lived through too much of this and pretended to understand
- ❖ People named John, Pat, Dwight and Tammy for their editing and encouragement
- ❖ All the interesting people I worked with for 32 years

Illustrations by Micah Miller and Jake Andrews, RBHS students

Published by:

PWJ Publishing
Post Office Box 238
Tehama, CA 96090

Names and identities have been changed to protect anyone who might be innocent. Use of actual names 5has been with the consent of those involved.

ISBN 0-939221-19-5

DRAWERS FULL OF STUFF

TOP DRAWER

SPARTANS RULE

Peluncony is a ▓▓▓

MIDDLE DRAWER

DRAWERS FULL OF STUFF

ANOTHER DRAWER

School
Sucks

XIII
XIV

BOTTOM DRAWER

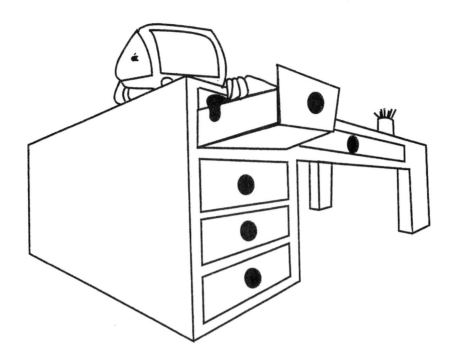

Top
Drawer

Stuff went into this drawer when Joe had too much hair and not enough patience. Some said these were very tough times for schools. Others said that it would have been a good deal for all concerned if Joe had decided to work in a winery.

M. B.

RIGHT UP FRONT

It's no surprise that Joe didn't turn out normal. I've known him forever and his upbringing was an unlikely mixture of baseball, the Beatles and la dolce vita. There's nothing normal about that recipe. So, years ago, I thought old Joe ain't gonna do well without his Brooklyn Dodgers ball cap and 'keep on truckin' Falcon panel wagon.

You take the nostalgic 50's innocence of Mickey, Willie and the Duke and throw in the hallucinogenic idealism of John Lennon. You've got a hippie at heart who lives for a perfect game. Just for fun, you add the uniquely Italian affliction compelling one to not take anything very seriously. A semi-normal and slightly eccentric wife and two semi-charming sarcastic daughters just add spice.

So early on I figured his first principal job wouldn't last long, even though it was in an alternative school for "at risk" misfits. He didn't ask for the job; he just had the keys after the principal retired. He survived for 12 years. Go figure. He always said it was like driving a garbage truck; no one gave him any crap because he had it all.

He left that job under protest. A new boss named him the 'interim' principal at a regular high school. Miraculously, he lasted there for 17 years. He succumbed to strange neckties, but otherwise seemed unaffected. Which is to say he disdained service clubs, golf and polyester but continued to enjoy kids, collect baseball cards, listen to the Beatles and go to Italy whenever he could. Pure luck gave him bosses who were talented and tolerant. He once said that he considered 'interim' the key to his longevity.

What follows is a random, rambling collection of what Joe felt like writing down or saving. Things that amused or confused him, he reduced to writing and stuffed in his desk drawers. Maybe it was 29 years of therapy, since he was amused and confused a lot. He wrote a column for the school paper, saved some student writings and other worthless souvenirs. It is a definitive representation of what he stuffed in those drawers, not much else. There is a wandering sequence, but any meaning or larger purpose is purely accidental. The pompous and paranoid, who recognize themselves and are ticked off, will have forgotten that he changed names and never let the truth ruin a good story. Or maybe they had it coming.

The reading does suggest that Joe probably did very little to change or revolutionize the educational system. On the other hand, there's not much evidence the system changed him either. He went out still loving kids and thinking most adults were OK. That's not normal. He should be real proud of that.

- Mickey Bitsko

Aw Nesta Gawd This Really Happened

It's the Principal of the Thing

There had been three principals in my professional life. Sister Gloria was a wonderful human being. She liked me. I was a nice young man teaching 7th grade, whom she thought hadn't wandered too far from his Catholic roots. I knew about holy water, confession and all that stuff. She had a constant, serene smile that I always thought must be hard to sustain with that tight black and white habit thing they all wore. We were quite cordial but didn't exactly do a lot of social things together, and there were more than a few things I didn't share with her.

One year later my principal was a dandy. Larry was a Labor Day loser, hired after the other guy left in a big hurry right before the start of school. An okay enough guy, Larry just hadn't been the same since a serious accident. This was his first job after a long rehab. Suffice to say, he did some weird things. They said he used to be semi-normal; it was the metal plate, the medication. He forgot things, he changed things, he had tantrums and routinely pissed off most everyone. Unfortunately, he had inherited a young, energetic, and somewhat sadistic staff. As junior high teachers, we mimicked junior high behavior at its worst. We talked about carrying magnets for the metal plate, stuff like that. It was not a pretty sight.

The Larry experience had me looking through Peace Corps brochures. The next year, I was fortunate to land in an alternative school, with just me, the crusty old principal and a roomful of rejects and delinquents. Floyd was a great guy. He looked like a real principal. He had done it all and was moved down to this job after serious heart surgery. We were together for two years. In between fish stories and retirement plans, Floyd taught me a lot about surviving in the system. This was good stuff, since I was in my third school in three years. My uncle's winery seemed to be the next stop.

In fact, I respected the guy so much, I even took administrative courses just because he said I should. If anyone else had suggested I take classes that at the time I considered God-awful torture, I'd have told them to go to hell. I may have even cut my long hair if he'd asked. Then Floyd retired. By default, I had his job. I was still teaching most of the time, the kids were challenging, everything was cool, except people were beginning to call me 'principal.'

So there I sat, with absolutely nothing in common with any of the other three who had the same title. Gloria had her rosary beads, Larry his therapist and Floyd, 100 years of experience. One way or another, they had paid their dues. For better or worse, they deserved the title. No kid ever snickered or said 'far out' when they were introduced as the 'principal.' I was only 27 years old, I didn't need the inevitable bureaucratic abuse that was forthcoming. I had friends who wouldn't understand. I imagined my old high school principal having a seizure if he found out at my 10 year class reunion.

I finally decided I could handle everything but the title. I cut my hair a little promised myself I'd keep quiet. A lot of friends of mine had lived through Vietnam, so I knew I could do this. After all, it wasn't a normal school, so I didn't have to be a normal principal. But I kept flashing on my own dufus high school principal and what we all said about him. Then there was Gloria and her serene smile, wacko Larry, and Floyd, who they named the damn school after when he retired. I didn't relate real well to these visions.

When you get right down to it, I guess it was just the principal of the thing. I'd either get over it or head back to the wine country.

"Great principals don't do great things.
Great principals get a lot of other people
to do great things"

- Mickey Bitsko

Excuse Me! 'My mare's in heat and I had to stay home to keep an eye on the neighbor's jackass.'

Principal Thoughts   *Bluffer*

Why Principals Wear Neckties

Have you ever really looked at a necktie? It doesn't cover your body. It doesn't keep you warm. It just hangs there; always getting in your soup or something. You can go to Macy's and spend $75.00 on one of these cloth things that squeeze your neck and have no practical use. For $75.00 I once bought a car - and it ran.

Yet nearly every male principal wears a tie all the time while at work. Why? Probably for the same reason we don't have nude centerfolds in The Bluffer. It has to do with what our audience expects and practical self-censorship.

The public who deals with a principal expects, in fact demands, a certain appearance. I could come to school in shorts and a tank top, but I'm sure teachers, parents, even students, would gasp and tell me exactly what I should wear. If I were a truly great principal, Dr. Panucci might pick out or censor my clothes every day before I came to school. It would be a lot better if I could be sensitive to my audience and do my own censoring.

I hear hundreds of compliments on the content and quality of The Bluffer. Occasionally, I get calls about articles that people feel are insensitive to a part of its readers. These callers usually want me to censor the student paper.

I will never pre-read or censor a student newspaper. First Amendment Rights are sacred and to be honored. Bluffer censorship sounds about as much fun as Dr. Panucci picking out my clothes.

The Bluffer has an audience that includes parents, elementary schools, senior citizens and high school students. This audience is somewhere between Sesame Street and Saturday Night Live. Student journalists need to clearly understand this audience, its expectations and values. This is one of journalism's most important lessons.

Being irresponsible and oblivious to readers will guarantee the loss of credibility and part of the vast audience The Bluffer has worked so hard to attain. Through mailing, delivery, supplies and equipment, journalism has received tremendous District support. We can't afford to offend too many people at District expense.

Besides, offending and shocking people is too easy. Any fool can do it. Skill, hard work and a keen perception are needed if you really want to inform, move and/or entertain people. Those who want to be shocked or offended will read Hustler or the National Enquirer.

This is not to say that The Bluffer needs to shun controversial issues or be a bland song dedication tabloid. In fact, nearly all negative calls are not criticizing content, only word choice. Overall, it is a great student publication. It is just that sometimes you just have to wear a neck tie - or you might get hung with one.

P.S. Did you notice the other day I wore a sweater and turtle neck? Don't tell Dr. Panucci.

*   *   *

AGONY
The old man screamed for mercy
As the pain contracted
Leaving him lifeless,
Giving him his wish . . .
The young boy screamed at his mother
As if in agony,
About having to do his homework
On Saturday.

-Robert

Excuse Me! 'I'm sorry Lee missed school again. Our car is a piece of junk.'

Aw Nesta Gawd This Really Happened

Mountain Mike

Mike could best be described as a combination mountain man/cowboy. At 6'2", 190 pounds, with bushy hair, boots and a large black cowboy hat, Mike commanded one's attention. With his heavy beard and a chaw of tobacco in his mouth, it was easy to understand how this 16 year old could get served in any bar in town. At school, he was shy, self-conscious and spoke infrequently in his slow drawl. He was generally polite, even though it was no great secret that he hated schools, teachers and flatlanders in general.

Mike was on probation for vandalizing mountain cabins near his home and also for being caught with 160 trout in his possession. At the regular high school, he was known as being quiet fighter, having terrible attendance and having few academic skills. He came to us after an incident at his bus stop in the mountains. As the story goes, there were four boys bleeding and licking their wounds when the bus arrived. Defending his little sister's honor (which apparently was a fulltime job), Mike had kicked the crap out of all four without even getting his hat knocked off. That had not been his first fight at the bus stop. Ironically, the bus stop is in front of the tavern where Mike's father, when home from the woods, carried on regular fisticuffs.

The first time I met Mike, he politely told me he never met a teacher he liked, not even a little. They were all pussies, big on book learning, but real stupid shits when it came to things that mattered - like doing an honest day's work. Months later he was to compliment me by saying that he doubted that I ever went to college, since I wasn't as stupid as other teachers he'd known.

As far as I knew, Mike's only interests were bull riding in the summer rodeo circuit, hunting, fishing, trapping predators and selling the furs. I knew nothing about rodeos, but had spent a lot of time in the outdoors as a kid. He was blown away that I said I knew how to track animals, skin a deer and stretch a hide. I'm not sure he believed much of what I said, but with me doing most of the talking, we developed a cautious relationship.

I first suspected that he was beginning to trust me when he started attending regularly, did some school work and didn't refuse to play on our softball team. I have never seen a kid so out of place doing school work. It was humorous to watch, as if his big grubby hands didn't belong around a book. Softball was even funnier. He could hit like a mule, but the sight of him rounding the bases in his boots and hat was hilarious. However, no one laughed. It should be noted that after one ugly collision at home plate, Mike generally ran the bases uncontested.

Even though he was becoming a staff favorite (we called him Sasquatch in faculty meetings), we were careful not to compliment himon whatever successes he had in school. Mike equated teacher praise with being called a kiss ass or worse. It became an unwritten agreement - "I'll do a little bit of this crap, but don't make it look like I need or like it."

One day after school, Mike awkwardly came up to me and drawled ""Are you too frickin' old to walk?" A bit surprised at the question, I told him I could probably still put one foot in front of the other for awhile. He responding by saying, "If ya' can walk, I'll show ya' the best trout fishin' ya' ever seen." I told him he had a deal. I then wondered what the hell I was getting myself into.

The next afternoon, Mike and I skipped out early and made the 40 mile trip into the mountains. He didn't say more than ten words all the way, except when we got near his house and he started pointing out places where he had killed deer or had trap lines set. We pulled into the front yard of the small wood frame house and were surrounded by barking dogs and rusting parts of logging equipment. His mother greeted us at the door. She was a small woman and worked at the local diner. He obviously had not mentioned my coming, since she was real nervous and kept running around picking up things from the floor and offering me coffee.

Mike went somewhere to gather his fishing gear, so I was alone with his mom. She showed me the living room wall photos of Mike bull riding. She told me Mike had made nearly a thousand bucks last year on the rodeo circuit, both riding and doing odd jobs. She also got out of the closet some beautiful furs from Mike's winter trap line. Since her old man leaves a lot, she said Mike's rodeo and fur money really helped.

Mike came back with his pole, creel and worms. As we headed out the door he grabbed two cold beers out of the refrigerator. He kissed his mom and told her he loved her. She didn't ask where we were going or when we'd be back. I wished she had, so I would have known. In fact, I don't think she even asked who I was.

We got in my truck and headed up a dirt logging road behind his house. Mike was talking all the time now. I was shy and self-conscious. We crossed a power company ditch that he said they had drained last spring. He said he had never been so pissed as the day he came by and found only small potholes of water full of dying trout. The stupid bastards were cleaning the ditch and killing all the trout in one of the best fishing spots around! Mike scooped up and carried in his coat as many trout as he could; better in his mom's freezer than coyote food he reasoned. The game warden who stopped him said he had l60 trout in his possession.

We also passed a group of cabins, the same cabins he had vandalized. He told me how one of the cabin owners had tried to make a citizens arrest on him during deer season for trespassing. Mike said he'd hunted there since he could walk and so had his dad and grandpa. Now these idiots from L.A. had come up here and bulldozed roads that slid into the creeks, built cabins and generally screwed up the country. They spent two weeks a year there, doing two years' damage with their kids' .22's and motorcycles. He showed me the spot where he'd found a yearling doe shot with a .22.

He told me how he and a friend had sure tore the hell out of the cabins after they'd broken in and drank most of their liquor. He showed no remorse and said they would have never been caught if his dad and uncle hadn't been bragging about it at the tavern.

He told me to pull over and park right in front of an ominous "No Trespassing" sign. We grabbed our gear and headed for a small spring where Mike put the cans of beer in the cold water. He then started stretching out his long legs at a trying pace.

Mike made little noise as we hiked a quick mile through tall pines. It was tiring but easy going with the smell of the trees and sounds of the animals to enjoy. I had to keep one eye on Mike, since he often froze in his tracks and then pointed out a deer bounding through the woods. On several occasions he stopped and squatted to examine tracks that had crossed the trail. He said nothing and I didn't say that I was beginning to wonder where the hell this creek was.

We finally came to a gorge that headed almost straight down. The walls of this canyon were covered with thick brush and large boulders, and if I listened very carefully, I thought I could hear a creek faintly roaring at the bottom. I began to wonder if maybe I wasn't "too frickin' old to walk."

Mike headed straight down, following a deer trail that tunneled through the thorny buck brush and around the lava boulders. Much of the time we were hunched over, but this didn't seem to slow Mike much. He stopped only once on the way down and that was to kill a rattlesnake with a rock. He didn't say a word about the snake, but I found the quick pace a bit easier after seeing the snake. The roar of the water was getting louder.

I was relieved when we reached the creek, only to find that Mike went immediately upstream. I asked him why we weren't fishing and he explained that we needed to cross the creek, since it was easier to fish from the shady side. The creek looked like a cover on Outdoor Life. It was just deep and swift enough to keep one from wading across as the white water cascaded into crystal clear pools where you could see trout swimming in schools.

A ways upstream we reached a 12 inch tree that had fallen across the creek. It was about 15 feet above the rushing water. Mike ran across it. I started to follow, but it was slick from all the mist, and I ended up crawling across on all fours. I hated doing that and it was even worse when I saw him impatiently waiting with a smirk on his face. I must have looked as foolish as he did with a book in his hand.

We were now ready to fish. Mike headed downstream, flicking his line into the pools, rarely failing to land a fish on the slightest nibble. I had never seen anyone fish with such intensity. He would creep up to a pool, toss out his line and remain completely motionless until something happened. Using a fly rod, he did not hold the line taut with his left hand; he actually put it in his mouth, allowing it to slip through his lips.

I was also catching fish and throwing back ones I thought too small. I decided the hike was worth it and then noticed that Mike was nowhere to be seen. He was downstream somewhere. It was then that I realized that the sun was long gone from the canyon and that there was no way anyone would hear someone yell. I kept fishing as darkness crept into the canyon.

I was telling myself that Mike would have to cross at the fallen tree and that I could probably find my way out anyway, even though it was now almost completely dark. I tried to remain real casual when Mike finally showed up. I asked him how many fish he had and he said it was bad luck to count them, even though his creel was obviously heavier than mine.

Following his lead, I began to clean my fish. I suggested we clean them at home, since it was so dark I couldn't see where to stick the knife. He said not to hurry, since the moon wouldn't be up for a while yet. Sure enough, about the time we finished cleaning the fish, the moon was visible at the rim of the canyon. Even though the full moon made it rather light, the tree crossing was a hairy experience, even on all fours. The hike out of the canyon set my lungs afire and showed me muscles I didn't know I had. The last mile on level ground seemed like a breeze.

We reached the beers and then sat on my pickup tailgate to enjoy them. Mike was now again back to talking, pointing to where he killed a five point buck he'd tracked for three straight days. He promised to show me the horns when we got back to his house.

I got home about midnight and flopped into bed. Getting up and going to school the next day was even harder than the hike out of the canyon, but there was no way I wasn't going to show up. Mike told me at school that he thought he'd go back that day and wanted me to go along. He just smirked when I said I had a meeting after school.

What Happened, JJ?

Dear who ever cares because I don't,

I was in class today a kid next to me said something about my mom and the word fart came to me so I said it. The teacher got mad at me for saying it so I sent to the office for saying fart. I think that the teacher that sent me to the office is a little old to be teaching. I don't like the guy in the first place. So I'm sitting in the office when this girl who is sitting next to me is telling me that her mom is a slut. Well before the bell rang Mr. Paliconione jump my ass for being in the office so much. Then he took me to his office and started to give me a lecture about how he has helped me. And how he had carried me under his wing and stupid shit like that. He said that I should start carrying him for the rest of the time. He told me that if I don't like it I could go home and find another school. Like Choices. But choices is for girls and guys that cant keep hands off each other and girls that get pregnant so I don't need to go there. God I cant stand this school hate it. I hate school period. I have no choice to go to school.

JJ

Excuse Me! 'I was late because a cop followed me to school and I couldn't go fast.'

Aw Nesta Gawd This Really Happened

JV Baseball and Marv

Coaching JV baseball at the regular high school was a good balance to spending most of the day at the school for the weird. These baseball players were not only happy and well fed, but had real live parents who cared about them. And when it came to baseball, they - especially the fathers - cared about them a lot.

They also cared who coached them and a scruffy haired newcomer wasn't their first choice. We got along just fine, but I sensed it was a tenuous relationship. I knew enough about baseball, loved the kids and, most importantly, they were a talented group, which translates to winning.   For me, it was thrilling to deal with parents whose biggest family trauma had been the extra inning loss to the Cottonwood All Stars.

Winning was no small thing. After all, with some of these very same dads as coaches, this group had been very successful Little League All Stars. So when this new coach moved Peewee, the Little League All Star second baseman, to center field, there was a perceptible rumble through the grandstands. Didn't this idiot know that Peewee had started two doubleplays against the Weaverville All Stars? We were winning, so no one said much to my face, but they definitely were on alert.

However, my credibility took a quantum leap upward when Marv showed up at practice. Marv Grissom, born and raised right here in Tehama County, had played a lot of years with the Giants. He'd pitched in World Series and All Star games and was currently a big league coach. He usually was Bill Rigney's pitching coach. Luckily for me, Rigney was canned as manager by the Angels or somebody, so Marv was out of a job and hanging around our ball park. I was impressed, especially when he offered to pitch batting practice.

Marv was not a chatty guy, but always had time for kids. My players (and dads) had great respect for Marv. I had his baseball cards and was in awe of the guy. I loved eavesdropping on his stories about Willie Mays and Ted Williams. He'd often bring a bat or something to practice that he'd used in the '54 Series and give it to some kid. I was horrified when the kid came to practice the next day saying he went home and hit rocks with it.

Marv pitched quite a bit of batting practice and one day asked if I minded if he worked with my pitchers. Would I mind if a big league pitching coach would take time with my JV goobers? I just hoped they wouldn't share too many stupid things I'd taught them. I'd played a lot of baseball, but the one time I'd pitched was in high school and the line drives up the middle almost killed me.

Prior to Marv, I got a lot of fatherly advice; after, nearly none. Marv had great style and timing. He'd watch kids throw, say very little and just make small adjustments and tell subtle and fascinating stories. He'd tell them about how he used to 'go up the ladder' with the fastball. He'd tell how Robin Robert's front foot would hit the ground at exactly the same release point on every single pitch. He'd never tell them to change anything, just how someone else got it done. The ones with ears improved immensely.

11

However, my favorite Marv story was about Billy, who, against my advice, threw his curveball with one finger knuckled. It had worked in Little League, against the Cottonwood All Stars, but was now getting whacked. In his dry, slow style Marv told Billy "I've seen about 300 pitchers hold the curve that way. Larry Jansen, a great pitcher who pitched in Series and All Star games, held it that way." After a pause, he added, "the other 299 weren't worth a shit and you're no Larry Jansen." Billy dropped the knuckle.

We won every game that year. I quit coaching soon after that. Some said it was because Rigney and Marv were hired by the Twins. Some said I was a poor sport and was afraid I might lose with next year's group. Others said that the dads had voted and I was out. None of that was true. It was actually the superintendent who told me that a principal had more important things to do. I've wondered about that ever since.

"The only way to prove you're a good sport is to lose."

- Ernie Banks

Excuse Me! 'Saw a doctor for my sore pitching arm; I write with it too.'

Aw Nesta Gawd This Really Happened

Dead Danny

Funerals are never fun, but this one had been worse than most. When I returned to school, I was wet, cold and had an ugly knot in my gut that wouldn't go away. I was alone in the building and for some reason decided to pull Danny's cumulative file. I looked at all the grade school photos of a cute little guy who had the same big grin from K to 8. The I.Q. scores were above average with five different elementary schools listed where teachers had written that Danny appeared "scrawny" or "undernourished."

The early elementary teacher comments all noted that Danny had been a happy youngster with friends, although often unkempt and dirty. They noted there was no father in the home and the mother was a no-show for parent conferences. The school nurse wrote that a second grade problem with sleeping in class was probably due to his mother working nights and Danny having to sleep in the car at her job site.

Junior high teachers noted he had "little supervision" and "ran with a rough crowd", but he was generally friendly and outgoing. A note by a counselor stated he was in a foster home while his mother was being "detained." High school grades were all F's. He was suspended different times for cutting, smoking and once for possessing marijuana. From the number of truancy notices, it seemed that he probably hadn't gone to high school many more times than that.

When I met him, Danny was still skinny, dirty and had the big grin. He had longish curly hair and always wore his shades. It was apparent that Danny drank, smoked, inhaled or injected most anything, but when confronted his pat response was that he was "high on life." His mother was a hopeless alcoholic and Danny pretty much did as he chose. Our alternative school was usually the only place his probation officer could find him, since he attended rather well. He was a pretty good student, well read and up on current affairs. He loved to hang around after school and argue most any point of view, especially if it appeared to upset the other person. He never lost his cool, relying on his quick wit to get him through most situations.

The accident happened about 3:00 A.M. Monday morning on a mountain road near Paynes Creek. All three of them were loaded on something. The car went over an embankment and rolled several times. There were no seat belts and all were thrown from the car. One was barely injured, another had serious injuries, including brain damage, while Danny was crushed by the car and killed instantly.

There were ten of us at the graveside service. Three were school friends. Danny's mother, reeking of alcohol, sobbed in the arms of a neighbor woman. Two funeral directors, Danny's probation officer and I served as pall bearers. A preacher was there to say a few words. It was only sprinkling when we got there, but was pouring before we got the economy casket in the grave. The funeral home hadn't put up one of those canopy things, so the preacher cut short the last reading. I think the knot in my stomach came from knowing that Danny had always been cut short.

Excuse Me! 'Randy's constipation made him a time bomb.'

Aw Nesta Gawd This Really Happened

Knife Fight

The investigating officer called me later the same afternoon wanting to make sure he had the facts straight regarding the noontime knife incident. Yes, both suspects were armed. One had his knife in his hand attempting to cause great bodily harm to the other. Yes, they each had threatened to kill the other. Yes, one of our teachers had single handedly disarmed both suspects. Yes, another teacher had chased and captured one of the suspects as he tried to flee the scene.

I asked the officer what they were being charged with and he responded that they were being cited for fighting in public, disturbing the peace, brandishing a weapon and assault with a deadly weapon. He quickly added that there was no place for these kinds in our schools and they'd see that they didn't see daylight for awhile. He noted that they both had prior records, and adults with priors and these kind of charges headed for the big house. I hung up the phone, sat back in my chair and thought about "these kinds," namely Henry and Gary.

Henry is round shouldered, stands about 5'4" in the work boots he wears every day. He has a boyish round face and a little pot belly over which he pulls his high water Big Mac pants. He also wears one of the grey and white striped work shirts with a zipper that he zips all the way to the top. Henry always smells kind of funny and is usually greasy, probably because of the oil throwing, thrashed motorcycle he drives to school. His oily hair is short and home cut. Henry wants to be a blacksmith.

Henry has few friends at school. The girls think he is a greasy nerd. I once heard him say something in shop that he thought was flirtatious. The little Indian girl responded quickly with a slap that knocked him clear off his stool and flat on his butt. He sobbed for the rest of that day and nearly every other kid in school took time to tease him. With his impish grin and good intentions, the teachers don't dislike Henry, but they certainly do try to avoid him. He's one of those kids who will follow a teacher around for an hour after school telling a boring and unbelievable story of how he almost killed the biggest buck ever seen in Tehama County.

In past years, Henry lived with his mother and they appeared to be real buddies, often joking and telling boring stories together. Their favorite story has to do with Henry's older brother being sent to prison on a bum rap. Neither ever mentioned Henry's father and Mom referred to Henry as her "little man." This school year, things seemed to be better for Henry - he had moved out of his home and was caretaker on a ranch about 20 miles from town.

Henry, indeed, does have a record. He is on probation for having scaled the fence at a local racquet club and stealing six tennis balls that had been left on the court.

Gary is a good looking kid with blond hair and Paul Newman blue eyes that wildly dart all over the place when you look at him. He stands about 5'3", is usually well dressed and appears younger than his 15 years. Gary rarely smiles, stutters badly and cries easily. He rides his motocross bicycle to school and is usually late.

He lives with his mother and stepfather now, but has spent most of his life being shipped back and forth between his mother and real father, a guard at Folsom Prison. His mother is often at school, usually blaming the school for having caused his weird behavior. I used to confront her with the possibility that Gary may, in fact, be responsible for some of his own behavior. She would then tell me that he must go back with his father, since he causes marital problems when he lives with her and she can't take it any longer. I've never met his father and the only time I mentioned him to Gary, he began crying and screamed "He hates me! He hates me!" His school file notes that Dad hangs up every time the school calls and he has never been to a parent conference. The whole family is well known to Mental Health.

Gary has no friends at school and usually sits by himself. Since he is mouthy and rarely turns in assignments, he is not a favorite with teachers. His behavior when corrected or confronted is very predictable. He first blames someone else and then cries. If the matter is pursued, he will throw a violent temper tantrum and run stammering and screaming from the building. He has done this at least six times and usually returns with his mother and then they both verbally assault whoever will listen - Mom screaming and crying, Gary stuttering and crying. The staff has been through these enough to know that their batteries eventually run down and they leave. It has been over a year since we have tried to reason with them.

Gary, too, is on probation. He was picked up recently, looking in a neighbor's window. The police charged him with whatever they charge peeping Toms with.

As far as I know, Henry and Gary have hated each other for years. They bicker at school daily and the only attention either usually gets from other students is when they are being egged on in their perennial feud. Last year at a school outing, they were fishing together and somehow Gary broke Henry's new fishing pole. Goaded on by the others, they tried to fight it out. When I got there, they were hugging each other and rolling around in the dirt, screaming obscenities at each other. No punches were thrown and neither was injured. It was all rather comical and I remember they both had little mud rivers running down their cheeks - a mixture of dirt and tears.

The knife incident was the culmination of a rather typical day in their relationship. Henry was working in the student store and as is normal, called Gary a puke for no apparent reason. Gary responded by leaning in the store window and spitting on Henry. Infuriated, Henry got out his old Scout knife and opened one of the bigger blades, a two incher with a rounded tip. He then told Gary that if leaned through the window again, he was going to cut his nose off. Gary sat down.

When finished in the store, Henry sought out Gary and proceeded to call him a string of unflattering words. It was now noon and students were putting books away. No one even noticed Henry and Gary hugging each other and again trying to fight. Finally, one of the teachers told them to knock that crap off and get the hell out of the building. They then went into the hallway, where they started to loudly scream at each other. When the teacher arrived, they were about ten feet apart and yelling that they were going to kill each other. Gary was crying and holding his small hunting knife. The teacher asked for the knife. Obviously relieved, Gary handed it over. Henry dug into his pocket and turned over his Scout knife. Gary then threw his temper tantrum and headed for the door. Another teacher ran out front, grabbed his shoulder and he fell to the ground and lay there sobbing. The students who had bothered to watch got back in the lunch line. Not wanting to talk to their mothers again, I called the police.

I wonder if Henry and Gary will go to the big house.

Write Me Your Biggest Trauma

"The most traumatic incident in my life was when my father walked out on my family. My father left us when I was almost four years old. I didn't know why he left me, he loved me so much."

- Bobby

"Once upon a time I used to be a little boy going to grammar school. I was just a little kid who had everything. Then it all changed because my mom and dad split up. I really didn't know what to think because I was just a kid. I always thought that parents were supposed to be together forever."

- Jared

"Of all things, I never ever thought my parents would split up. They never fought or anything. I always thought they seemed so happy. I was so sad. The worst thing was my two brothers and my sister were at a weird stage. They were old enough to understand, but too young not to have them together. They really needed a mom and dad. So did I."

- Vickie

Excuse Me! 'Claudia was absent yesterday because she had a dental appointment. It was a choice between school and a root canal and school lost out.'

16

It's the People, Stupid

John

John was the best teacher I ever saw. No teacher ever cared more about kids - smart ones, stupid ones, dirty ones, preppy ones - all kinds of kids. Never mind that he once threw a baseball bat at a kid on a motorcycle. The bat didn't hit him, the kid was an idiot and the biased witnesses agreed he had it coming.

John arrived at school early, ate lunch with kids and stayed late. It seemed that he lived at school. Never mind that I once took him to help recruit a female ag teacher and he whizzed right in front of her. They became good friends and she was a great ag teacher.

John always seemed to be slipping kids money, taking them home or putting them up for the night. Never mind that he once drove his old Chevy truck up to the back door of the county office and he and two kids loaded it with AV equipment. He swore they'd never miss it, since they never checked it out to anyone. He was right.

John would teach anything. He liked math best and kids who hated math wanted desperately to learn it simply because John wanted them to. He also coached swimming and his swimmers always swam a little faster than their ability warranted. Never mind that "asshole" was what he frequently called anyone who didn't share his passion for honesty, learning and hard work. The "A" word was not limited to kids, as discovered by more than a few pompous parents, cranky colleagues and grumpy community members.

John loved telling stories and could see the bright side of most any fiasco. He had a great sense of humor. Never mind that the joke was often on him. Like the time his shop class measured and measured, measured and sawed, measured and hammered and built a playhouse. It was beautiful, but a little too big to get it out of the building. Everyone, including John, laughed till they cried.

Graduates seemed to always come back and want to see John. He seemed to be everyone's most memorable, if not their favorite, teacher. Never mind that when John was given tenure, he threatened not to take it. He said only bozos needed tenure and he'd been a park ranger, sold insurance and done a bunch of other stuff. They could just tell him to leave if he wasn't doing the job. They never did. They also could not figure out how to take his tenure back.

John was a delight in parent conferences, since he reeked of sincerity, spoke his mind and made it obvious that he cared deeply about kids. Never mind that he had an extremely low tolerance for blamers, enablers and excuse makers. As a result, I sat in on more than a few exciting and memorable conferences.

One comes to mind. Lucinda was an attractive black girl whose mother came to me because John was "a white, honky prejudiced bastard" who "wouldn't listen to Lucinda's point of view on some missing money." I listened to her, calmed her down a bit and assured her that the three of us could sit down, express our points of view and rationally get through this misunderstanding.

I asked Lucinda's mom to speak first. She left out some of the expletives, but repeated that she thought John was prejudiced. John quietly listened while I added that I'd known John for years and that he was very fair and anything but prejudiced.

John cleared his throat several times. The veins in his neck popped out. I knew this was a prelude to his point of view. Very loudly, and directly, John said "You bet your ass I'm prejudiced." John paused and glared at the woman. I about died. He continued, "I hate liars and thieves. I don't give a damn what color they are - and neither does my Chinese wife. Call me if you want to talk about my prejudice against liars and thieves." John then got up and stomped out of the room.

To my surprise, Lucinda's mom was calm as we sat there looking at each other after John left. She said she'd talk to Lucinda about stealing. She also said that she didn't know why, but Lucinda had told her that John was her favorite teacher. I wasn't surprised.

I don't remember ever seeing the woman again. John was at school early the next day. Never mind that he had swim practice that morning.

Ode to Red Bluff

Take me home
Beer suckin' Daddy
Wipe your boots
With my hair

Tell me between spits
You really care
Sleep with my friends
Promise it will never end

Give me your rancid socks
To darn and mend
Breed me like a rabbit
Love me like your cousin,
Sister or something

Come over here
My Red Bluffian
Beer suckin' Daddy
You know I love you
More than beef, Baby!

- Sarah

Excuse Me! 'My chicken was sick and I stayed home with it. Actually, it was my uncle's best fighting rooster and he almost died.'

Jake was out sick all those day before Xmas.

James had a ~~knot~~ knot on his Head in the Back ~~down~~ down by his neck. the Doc. did not Know what it was or why it was there, they thought it may be because of never's bat were not sure. they gave him some pill's to take for it, but the pill's knoct him out. I could not get him awake for school (I could wake him up But he acted Like a drune and talked funny he would not stay awake he'd go back to sleep that's what I mean when I said I could not wake him up). He would wake up about 2:00 or 2:30 every day. the pill's he took were for the realy Bad Headcks he was haveing from the knot on his Head. I called the Doc. and told them the pill's were Knocting him out and He could not go to school. they said he could go to school. they would not under stand he would not wake up for school.

as soon as I can make them under stand this I can get a Doc. exyous for you, Right now they are saying he could have gone to school, I'm going in to day at 3:00 to see them in person to get this straint out.

—thank you

An All-Too-True Essay

Run, Run, Runaway

Amid screeching matches and slamming doors were the ever present cries to be free, independent and on my own. Away from all the crap and the guilty family ties, away from the need/want to have things the way they used to be, like before the divorce. And if it wasn't going to be that way, then I wasn't sticking around to find out the alternatives. Or so I threatened. But that defiant dream was a long time dying. Hanging around became easier as the fear of leaving became stronger. Finally, two weeks after my 12th birthday, and after a big fight, irrational and hurting, I left, one sock and shoe on, the others clenched in my fists. When the lock clicked, a bitterness, almost hatred settled in.

Being "free" and "on my own" was great . . . . for about a week. Then my filthy sweat-stained clothes and greasy hair became unbearable. Angry pride denied any suggestion of returning, though my skin's pores ached for a shower, and my body, drugged by loss of sleep, wanted desperately to sleep on a bed rather than the cold, hard cement. And maybe if enough time had passed under these conditions, I might have gone home, but the appearance of Angie and other "free" kids in similar predicaments led me to join this "free" group and show my mother what I was all about. And show myself, though it was a long time before I knew much.

I quickly learned many skills during my time with the bunch of kids. These included how to steal 'Snickers' candy bars and how to get people to buy us quarts of beer. Stealing and just the circumstances made me wary of every person who happened into my periphery. So when Angie asked if I wanted to go to the City with her, I wasn't afraid of actually being there, but of what might happen when we got there.

We left that day. Hitchhiking was a new experience to me then, but soon became a common way of traveling. We stood part way up the 'on' ramp in Walnut Creek, thumbs and hips out, trying to entice drivers to stop. About a half-hour later, some guy in a washed-out VW Bug stopped. "Sure I'm going to San Francisco. Hop in." So we did. Angie sat in the front seat, being the slick talker, and I in the cramped back seat. I have to admit I was nervous. In fact, I was scared to death. The whole trip, while Angie strung this guy out on some fantastic story about how both her parents had recently died and how my mother beat me with a whip, I kept remembering the times my mother had told me how dangerous it was to hitchhike. It wasn't the way it used to be, people just being friendly, helping each other out. Now bad things happened; people were killed, raped. Girls, especially girls. Dangerous. Panic rose in me and blocked out all sounds, voices, car engines, replaced by a loud hum in my brain.

The bright lights, fuzzy through the fogged window my face was pressed against, brought me back from my nightmares of what might happen to us to the reality that we were here. This was it. The Big Destination. I knew my way around San Francisco, but Angie knew better, and more important, had a specific place to go. I had never been to Castro Street before; both sides of the street were packed with people; the air was *electric with voices, conversations and propositions, heels clicking and various types of smoke.*

Crossing the street at l8th and Castro, we met Michael. They knew each other from somewhere. Michael worked at the Sausage Factory, a Greek and Italian restaurant and pizza parlor. The atmosphere was casual; there were antiques hanging on the walls, very stylish looking. A long, narrow strip lead to the Back Room. Here was a small bar and oven where the 'to go' pizzas were ordered, cooked and picked up. The jukebox there was always playing, sometimes people would dance, but there wasn't much room. It was here that Michael worked. He invited us in for a couple of drinks. We sat at the smallish bar while Michael poured beer after beer into our coke glasses. By the time everything was closed down and we were the only ones left, I was quite wasted. I can't remember where we slept that night or many nights after that. Sleeping wasn't a major concern; living was day to day and many times we didn't sleep at all. I remember once we slept in a friend's car. I was sore all over the next day.

Angie liked to go back and forth from the City to the East Bay and would stay a few days in each place. I went back to the East Bay with her once and it ended up being a joke, Angie once again pulling her disappearing act, leaving me standing alone in the Richmond Bart Station. So, mostly I stayed in the City close to Castro Street. Through Michael, I got to be pretty good friends with guys who worked there. Tony, the boss, asked me one day if I wanted an errand job, since I hung around the place so much. The job consisted of running errands for the guys and Tony. (To get a lemon for the eggplant if they ran out, cigarettes, etc.) But mostly the job was cleaning up glasses and ashtrays in the Back Room. I got free meals and menial pay. But it was something to do, and I enjoyed being around the guys. It also helped me forget that I had no place to go each night. Most of the time I stayed with Junior, a cook at the restaurant. We had become really good friends since that first night. I especially liked the fact that Junior never made advances and I was able to relate to him. Once I called my mom from Junior's apartment. She hung up.

Angie came back after a long time being gone. She wanted Michael to take us over to this sleazy hotel where she was supposed to meet some "friend" of hers. While I was talking to Michael in the car, she went up to this guy's room. She had told me that she would wait right inside for me, but when I came in, she wasn't anywhere to be seen. So I went around to each room and listened, trying to hear her voice through the doors. I went to each door twice and didn't hear her. So I went back to the lobby-like hallway and sat down on the stairs to wait for her. Little did I know she was staying all night.

During the three to four hours I sat on those stairs, a man in his twenties kept coming down and asking if I wanted to go to his room. I repeatedly said no. Finally, I don't know after how many times, he came down and asked me again. And again I told him to get lost. Only this time he got mad, and he slugged me several times in the face. When I got hold of myself, I got angry and slapped him. When I saw the look on his face, I thought he was going to kill me. He had massive hands, I remember, as they closed around my neck. I was stunned; I couldn't breathe. I remember his face, so close to mine, bulging, contorting, sneering. His dark eyes were blank. Finally, I reached up and grabbed his wrists, and as I dug my nails into his flesh, I brought my knee up as hard as I could in his groin. He let go and I ran out into the street.

It was about 4 in the morning and Mission Street was deserted. Sobbing, I sat down on a bench. Immediately, I noticed a car circling around the block. After the third time, I got up and took off, hiding in dark doorways. The car, black and low to the ground, was following slowly now. I wanted to scream, but my fear silenced me, and I crept around staying close to the walls and in the shadows. I kept trying to ditch this car containing potential killers, rapists. I didn't know what was in the slinky black car creeping down the street after me. I was positive I didn't want to find out either. Unnoticed before, a long brown Cadillac stopped right in front of the stoop in which I was pressed into. The passenger door opened and a friendly voice told me to get in. I don't know why I got in, it might have been the soothing voice or my desperation, but I did. He was tall, black and a pimp.

He took off his beige hat and told me to get down in the seat. I did. He turned off the car lights, and we glided through the streets silent except for the low hum of the engine. At last we stopped in front of a park; we had lost the evil blackness following me. He asked me what happened; I told him. Still, I was scared and I sat on the far edge of the seat, up against the door. I remember how shocked I was when he asked me if I was a girl. Why wasn't I wearing a dress he wanted to know. I shrugged. He didn't believe it; he thought I was a boy. I told him I wasn't. When he reached over and engulfed my breasts with his huge hand, I stiffened. And when he was satisfied I was indeed a female, he took his hands away. It was getting light out now. He told me to come back here, at the park, at 3 that afternoon and he would buy me more dresses than I'd ever seen. I got out of the car. I never saw Ricky the pimp again, but neither did I have the urge.

Bad things always happened when I was around Angie. My black eye and fat lip kept me away from her for a short time. But she was back again, and again I went along with her, playing her game. Only this time the stakes were higher. Angie wanted to go to this park. Who knows why? So we went. In the park we met these two guys. It seems now like Angie must have known them, but at the time I didn't notice. Angie and one of the guys took off to another part of the park. So there I was stuck with some guy I didn't even know. We ended up talking awhile; I can't remember about what.

After a short time we started looking around for Angie and her friend. Naturally, Angie had disappeared. The guy I was with assured me that he knew where they were and he would take me there. So we started walking to his friend's house. We just had to make a few stops here and there. The last stop took the longest. We went into this small room where an old man, wrinkled and worn, sat on as rickety wooden chair at a desk, rolling joints. They seemed to be good friends; they talked about things that were happening around. During all this they smoked a couple of joints together. I declined.

Finally, we left. It was dark when we came outside the old man's apartment. We walked for another half hour until we got to this huge, deserted-looking apartment building. Only it wasn't deserted. We climbed a flight of stairs to the second floor. All the doors were closed; we went in the door at the end of the long corridor. When he opened the door, there was, as promised, Angie. She was sitting on some guy's lap, opened the door, there was, as promised, Angie. She was sitting on some guy's lap, smoking pot. I looked around through the smoke filled room. The room itself was long and narrow with bay windows all around the end. There were about six guys in the room, most just sitting and talking. One was crashed out on a big pillow in the corner, his tongue hanging out of his mouth. I remember I just sat against the wall, inhibited and scared.

After a long hour or so, Angie jumped up and spoke quickly to some guy with a beard. The guy got up and Angie motioned for me to come with them. We left the room and went around the corner. Here, the guy took out a key ring and opened the door. The room was totally blue, a florescent blue, a color that made you sick to your stomach. I walked into the room, assuming that's what I was supposed to do. Before I turned around the door shut, and as I was turning around, he locked it. I heard it click.

I was alone with the guy with the beard. He told me this was where I would be sleeping tonight, in this blue room. Suddenly, he was pressed against the front of me, the wall against my back. A loud knocking on the door stopped his pressuring body. He opened the door and everyone who had been standing in the long room, including the guy who had crashed, was standing in the corridor. They were going to the store one of them said, did we want to go or stay? The guy with the beard's answer drowned out my small mouse answer that, yes I wanted to go. Okay, they said, and as they all went out the door, the beastly-looking bearded guy grabbed my arm and yanked me into the room and locked the door. He came towards me, monster size, crushing me against the wall.

I pushed and shoved; he was like a lead weight, massive, solid, insulting. When he ripped my shirt off, I clawed his face, his arms, his chest. He picked me up and put me down on the floor, the dirty shag carpeting rough against my cheek. I screamed and screamed. No one came. My pants became shreds of clothing thrown aside. All I could hear was my heart and this monster's bursting breath. It hurt bad.

The only good thing was I wasn't even old enough to get pregnant. All I could think of was why did she have to hang up?

*   *   *   *

Family

Never had one all mine
Shared with with my brothers
Shared it with my sisters
But never had one all mine.

Alicia

Excuse Me! 'Yesterday I ran away. Please don't tell my parents I'm back.'

23

Said and Meant

Principals are rarely afforded the opportunity to tell parents exactly what they think. Since safety and survival usually supercede honesty, they often veil the ugly truth that I often found right on the tip of my tongue. This self-imposed censorship and distortion of the truth is an art form for administrative survivors. Some examples:

Said: "School is not easy for your son."
Meant: "He is stupid as a post."

Said: "Your daughter is very social and the consequences concern me."
Meant: "Get her on birth control."

Said: "His mood and behavior changes are confusing to us."
Meant: "He's doing a lot of drugs."

Said: "He is often very frustrating to his teachers."
Meant: "They hate him."

Said: "Your consistent concern and interest for your son is appreciated."
Meant: "Your constant complaining is a pain in the ass."

Said: "There is some confusion as to what actually happened."
Meant: "Your kid is a damn liar."

Said: "The competition for cheerleading is very keen."
Meant: "There are no fat and ugly cheerleaders."

Said: "Yes, theft at school can be a problem."
Meant: "Your irresponsible son would lose his head if it wasn't attached."

Said: "I'm sorry, but I must go now; I have a 2 o'clock meeting."
Meant: "I'm real tired of your bull. Don't let the door hit you in the rear."

Said: "We have some wonderful alternative programs."
Meant: "We are about to throw your kid out of school."

Said: "I agree that the teacher should express his concern differently. "
Meant: "Your kid *is* an asshole."

Excuse Me! 'My mother got religion and thinks I shouldn't go to your school.'

24

Aw Nesta Gawd This Really Happened

A Home Visit

Bobby seemed eager to attend school, but it was the third time in a week he'd cut school. He was hard to figure out, average in skills, but something was missing. He had a blank stare, frazzled hair and weird clothes not unlike Kramer on the TV show, Seinfeld. He lived near the school, so Dick and I decided to make a home visit.

We drove up, got out of the car and were instantly assaulted with the stench of dog shit. A skinny, rib showing doberman and several other mutts growled and snarled inside the not-too-sturdy fence. We could see some people in the back of the dilapidated house, which needed paint and had at least two broken windows. We walked along the fence, down the alley to where they were. Bobby was in the back yard working on his bicycle. We could barely hear him over the dogs when he introduced us to Phil. He was a skinny guy in his mid-twenties, with many tattoos, wearing a dirty T-shirt with "huevos" across the front. He smiled and you couldn't help but notice that his brown teeth were intermittent, at best.

From outside the fence, we tried asking Bobby why he had cut school, but Bobby kept looking at the ground, the dogs kept barking and growling while Phil was screaming at the dogs to shut up. In the meantime, a small, adult male was sneaking out the back door and watching the commotion. He was hunched over with darting eyes. He possessed an intense hunted look. He had a butch-style haircut and it looked like big chunks had been pulled out. He made loud grunting sounds that we could hear over the dogs. He was special, but Bobby and Phil pretended like he wasn't even there.

Shortly afterward, a grossly overweight woman rambled out the back door. Wearing a brownish white tank top, purple polyester slacks and flip-flops, she had crude tattoos on both of her large arms. She had a very short haircut. I couldn't help but looking at the oblong globs of fat that were squeezed out of her tank top and hung under her arms like small watermelons. She was not an attractive sight. She looked directly at Dick and me and was not smiling. Then her loud voice immediately got everyone's attention and even calmed the dogs.

She began a long, confusing monologue. She rambled on about social security checks, Phil going back to jail, drugs, what a hassle the retarded are and that Bobby was no better than the worst of them. Phil and the hunted guy stood quietly and looked right at her. Bobby just kept looking straight down at the ground and fiddling with his bike. He said nothing.

Although Dick and I never said a word to each other, we both knew we did not want to see the next thing that might come out of that house. So when the fat lady slowed down a bit, we thanked them for something and abruptly left. We did not have any idea why Bobby cut school.

Excuse Me! 'My aunt was supposed to give me a ride, but she accidentally got drunk.'

Aw Nesta Gawd This Really Happened

Interim Principal

The Board had appointed me 'interim' principal. No one, including me, had any idea what 'interim' meant. I was sort of a body to fill a void until the District figured things out. Okay with me, they were paying well. It was summer vacation and the only people around school were the maintenance and custodial folks, who must have thought 'interim' meant crazy. I had little idea what I was doing, but figured 'interim' must have meant 'get something done in a hurry, since you'll be gone real soon.'

If they didn't think I was crazy, they at least felt very sorry for me. I didn't understand anything about government work and school maintenance.   These were good enough people, but they definitely had government jobs. The unwritten code - 'Don't work hard enough to finish any job early or show up a fellow employee.' 'That will only get you more work, less overtime and no additional employees.'

I was clueless. All I could see was the dingy/shabby/dirty campus where everything was *almost* clean, repaired or repainted. I asked the stupidest questions, like 'Why is the lawn dry?' Well, dummy, 'It's dry because when we water it, ants come out of the ground and we have no ant poison and no one to apply it if we did.' Oh!

So when I asked them to tear down the semi-temporary and permanently ugly walls dividing the main office and to paint the classroom doors before school started, the head guy told me they had mowing (why would they mow dry grass?) and waxing schedules, but they *might* get to some of it.   I waited a week, saw no sign of action and then got crazy. I figured interim guys can do that, since 'interim' means you are already fired; you just don't know when. I yelled at the maintenance guy and he said he'd try to free a man. Sure enough, the next day, one of the guys painted four doors. I was told that there were 65 doors and it would take three weeks and that my obsession was going to leave floors scuffed.

The next morning I put on my old clothes, arrived early, got the paint, roller and brush and hit the hallways. I didn't stop to eat and don't remember even going to the bathroom. Before the crew had finished their afternoon break (which was akin to a religious interlude), I had painted 21 doors. I then headed for the office and started kicking and smashing the tacky veneer walls and down they came - in about 20 minutes. I threw the trash in front of the office. I went home covered with blisters and paint. My body was thrashed, but I had a good feeling, knowing that I had accomplished something during my 'interim' assignment.   My wife assured me that 'interim' meant this had been my last day.

The next day, the crew quietly hauled away the trash outside my office. Miraculously, the rest of the doors got finished in the next two days. No one ever said anything to me, but after that, they never looked at me quite the same.

A few of those guys still work for us. They are great employees with 'get it done' attitudes - and none of them is 'interim.'

Excuse Me!   'The strap on my artificial arm broke.'

Aw Nesta Gawd This Really Happened

The Plum War

When I first took the job as principal of a large high school, I did not have a clue as to how problems and the failure to solve them are the life blood of bureaucracies. Committees, studies and task forces conveniently direct the energy away from the problem. I also did not appreciate that impulsive insanity is often the best remedy. The Plum War was my awakening.

There was this plum tree right in the middle of campus. Every spring, it was loaded with little purple plums. It didn't take a doctorate in adolescent behavior to predict that teenagers would relish hitting each other on the side of the head with these juicy morsels. Not only that, most were poor shots who accidentally pelted the buildings, teachers and anything else within range. Teenagers with a pocket full of plums lurked behind every corner. Walking through the campus was an adventure. Special bulletins and detentions heightened the thrill.

This annual ritual had to have taken place ever since the large tree began bearing fruit, and I doubt if it ever had a lousy crop. I soon discovered that the Plum War created a special bureaucratic event rivaled in generating complaints only by cheerleader tryouts. Parents sent me complaints about stained clothing; teachers sent me complaints about plums in the classroom; the head maintenance guy sent me complaints about shoddy supervision; custodians complained to anyone who'd listen and the war raged on.

Now, I imagine in the past most of these complaints were answered. They may have even appointed committees and task forces to study the problem. I'm sure what happened was that plum season only lasted a few weeks and eventually everybody's blood pressure returned to normal and no one thought about it for another year. The task force never met and the problem went away.

I spent several days fielding complaints, doing more supervision and dodging plums. All I had to show for it was a stained sports coat. I knew something was wrong when I found myself wanting to throw a plum at somebody - ANYBODY! Then, on a Saturday afternoon, sitting at home, it hit me. I had to be the stupidest bureaucratic idiot in the world. The solution was obvious.

I put my chain saw in my old pick up and headed for school. The firewood was excellent and not one person ever asked me what happened to the plum tree. The Plum War was over and we were going to have to think of something else to do for two weeks next spring.

Excuse Me! 'I got female problems in my stomach. You wouldn't know about that.'

27

Just Plain Crackers

Nunya

She was rather pretty, with short blonde hair and blue eyes. She was new to our school and seemed to be pleasant enough and quite articulate. However, she came with a file several inches thick, had been institutionalized a number of times and was said to be prone to violent outbursts. Our very professional psychologist said she was 'crackers.' Nonetheless, she seemed rather normal for her first few days of school.

I was in my office doing whatever principals do at nine in the morning when I heard a horrible commotion outside my door. The new girl was screaming that she was going to kill her teacher. She was using very colorful and descriptive language that included knives, blood and many four letter words.   Every time the school psychologist approached her and tried to calm her, she screamed "Don't look at me , bitch!" loud enough to be heard all over the building.

Well, I had Psych IA in college and couldn't very well ignore this performance, since the secretaries were in various stages of shock. So, I calmly approached her and invited her into my office. I asked her to be seated and closed the door. She complied and as I took a seat next to her I remembered that I had in fact gotten an 'A' in that psych class. She was smiling as she slowly looked around at the pictures in my office.

Then in my most soothing voice and calmest manner, I asked her what her name was. She replied "Nunya" in a very soft voice. I wasn't sure if I had heard her correctly so I softly asked, "Nunya?" She politely answered "Yes, Nunya." Thinking I had it right I then inquired, "Nunya what?" Her blue eyes turned steely cold as she glared at me for a second and then screamed "NUNYA FUCKING BUSINESS!"

Since Nunya's act had sent a kind of 911 shock wave through the building, one of the vice principals was peering in my window. I thought he needed to experience this one, so I motioned him in. He came in sat down and I told him to ask her what her name was. He asked her and she replied sweetly, "Connie, what's yours? You have beautiful blue eyes." I don't even think he took Psych IA.

Someone, who probably had Psych IB, had called the parents and they soon arrived. They took Nunya to Mental Health. She was definitely 'crackers.'

"Often it does seem a pity that Noah and his party did not miss the boat."
- Mark Twain

Excuse Me! 'Marty didn't go to school for two days because one of the teachers kicked him out of class and he got mad and every time he gets mad he gets sick, so he had fever for two days and bad headaches.'

Teen Truth at Ground Level

Walking around campus with my head down is something I do. People probably assume I am in deep thought. Actually, I am looking for discarded bits of reality, in the form of teen notes disguised as trash. It is apparent to me that the best source of teen truth can be found under foot. Most of the notes have to do with the eternal triangle, simple primitive love notes or detail some forbidden activity. Many of them use language that would get them grounded at home and thrown out of class at school. The notes keep me current and provide a glimpse into that secretive teen subculture that few teens share with old people. Not unlike the Mafia, teens use school itself as a legitimate front to mask what is really going on. Grades, textbooks, courses of study and other important looking stuff is like the upstanding garbage business that only makes us wonder what the Mafia is really up to. Maybe the FBI should check if Godfathers write dirty little notes and inadvertently drop them on the ground.

Wendy

Please don't laugh at me when I ask you this question. What would you do if, I said I liked you, or if I could see you in a pair of blue pro Rodeo Wranglers Befor school is out.

I have liked you for a long time. I like your eyes and your hair and you.

Just because we listen to differnt kinds of music don't mean a thing to me. You know this is the longest letter I even wrote a girl.

So tell me true. what is your answer O. K.

Excuse Me! 'I had to go to Reno with my Mom in case she had a flat. My brother had to go in case she had two flats. The tires are really bad.'

Aw Nesta Gawd This Really Happened

Horrible Howard

There are so many good teachers. There are also a few memorable morons. One of my biggest fears is that long after I'm gone, someone will be asking, "Who was principal when they hired this idiot?" Howard is one of those guys. Howard is also not his (or her) real name and he is also a composite of a number of idiots. Because if Howard knows anything, it is the phone number of the teacher union lawyer. Paranoid and vindictive, he could read this somewhere. I don't need to be sued again.

Not all of us in education are brilliant, but most are well educated and know our limitations. Howard doesn't know that he doesn't know. He can be counted on to prolong every faculty meeting, asking the stupidest question. I once offered a nice prize for whoever asked the stupidest question. We voted and he won. If I'd sent a subtle message, he didn't get it. He loved it. It was a dumb idea. I didn't do it again. He's also the "what if" champion. He loves serving on the District's safety committee. What if a shot from the intruder's Uzi takes out the intruder alarm system? What if a Mt. Lassen eruption strands a school bus load of kids in a sea of molten lava? What if the principal hired a hit man for Howard? Oops, that last one is mine.

Howard's also a big shot in the union. He has no respect from his peers, but there's rarely a long line of folks for those jobs. It gives him status. How else could this idiot saunter into the principal's office, plop down and share his 'what ifs?' His title gets the principal to feign attention, at least till he's out the door. Howard did okay as union president, reelected several times, in fact, until there was an issue. With something at stake, he managed to divide the faculty, misrepresenting all concerned parties. They impeached him, which had to be a first. It was only a bump in the road, he's back on the sunshine committee or something.

Howard's a disaster in the classroom. Kids dislike him a lot and the counselors have learned to avoid placing kids with parents who care in his classes. It's just easier that way. I'll even admit to pulling rank and getting my own daughter out of his class. I couldn't stand her and her mother's diatribes at the dinner table every night.

He's into rigid rules, dittos and questions at the end of the chapter. He teaches the same subject all day. He's horrible. One year, I set a goal to teach him how to teach. We had a conference. I'd do a lesson first period. He'd observe and video tape me; we'd discuss it during his prep period. He'd then follow the model. I did my homework and had a perfect lesson. We reviewed the tape together, I shared the lesson plan, pointed out the 5 point steps of a good lesson, blah, blah. He seemed enthused. The next day - I'm not making this up - he showed his classes the video of me. First period bitched because they'd seen me live the day before. He reported the other classes liked it. I almost cried.

He has tenure. We won't fire him. Who was principal when they hired the idiot?

Excuse Me! 'No one should have to go to a class where you're smarter than the teacher.'

Aw Nesta Gawd This Really Happened

Riley

I guess you just had to have been there. There is no way you describe the feeling in the gym that day when Riley won the lip synch contest. Riley is in our severely handicapped class. He is not much over four feet tall, but a real presence on campus. He'll usually give me a high five when I meet him in the cafeteria every day and then say "Adios, amigo" as he leaves. Despite his handicaps, Riley is one of the most cheerful kids at school.

The lip synch contest was a traditional event during Homecoming week and had entries from all parts of the school. They included the cheerleaders, homecoming queen candidates, FFA group, football players, several others and Riley. The preliminary competition was a lunch time activity held near the cafeteria. Riley was certainly the most serious candidate and had probably rehearsed his act the most. The teachers serving as judges declared Riley the winner. You could have expected it. He was good and empathetic teachers would do the right thing.

This gave Riley his big shot at the homecoming rally Friday afternoon. Donning a western shirt, wranglers, boots and one of those huge foam cowboy hats, Riley ambled to the center of the gym floor. He reached out and asked the student body president for the mike. The crowd grew silent.   Riley is not easy to understand but everyone heard him when he squinted through his thick glasses at his wheel chair bound girlfriend, Becky, and announced that he was dedicating this song to her.

Alabama's '*Why, Baby, Why'* came blasting over the sound system. Riley began his animated tapping of his boot to the instrumental introduction, while strumming on the oversized guitar he carried. This was no ordinary event at a high school rally, which is a showcase for the best, brightest and prettiest. Every adult in the gym wondered how the youth of America was going to receive one of its own who wasn't so endowed.

When Riley put his head back and contorted his face on the first vocal notes, the roar was deafening. Hands above their heads, 1500 teenagers began swaying in unison to the music. As he came to the end of the song, the crowd rose to their feet with the loudest ovation that gym had ever heard. He waved to Becky and left the floor with his arms above his head and his fingers in a V sign, with the crowd chanting 'Ri-ley!, Ri-ley!, Ri-ley!' No adult in the place had a dry eye. Riley was great - and the youth of America wasn't bad either.

"Life isn't always fair, but it's good. Never give up."

- Bethany Brownfield

Excuse Me! 'I stayed up all night writing my English paper and then fell asleep in my car in the parking lot this morning.'

RED BLUFF

FOOTBALL

Dear Spartan Fans,

All across America, high schools are beginning another football season. It's a uniquely American experience, complete with bands, pom-poms and flags. All schools produce a football program. All of the programs have a 'message from the principal.'

But does anyone ever read the 'message?' Of course, the principal thanks the supporters and wishes the team well. So do I. But does the 'message' do anything but take up space that could have been used for a photo of last year's Section champs?

I can't remember ever reading a 'principal's message' and I've seen hundreds of programs. I would love to meet someone who really does read the 'principal's message.' In fact, I'll buy one of those great FFA tri-tip sandwiches for the first person who approaches me at a game and says they have actually read it.

Have another great season Spartans!

Sincerely,

Joe Pelanconi
Principal

Note: At the third (yes, *third*) home game, a little grey haired lady approached me and said she had read my 'message.' She loved the tri-tip, but said she read it because she hated watching football. Her grandson played.

Autumn

It has always puzzled me how some youngsters who have struggled to succeed, can't stand success. They do something stupid. They confuse pain and pleasure. Just before graduation, Autumn gave me this poem after she had run away for no apparent reason.

The Pleasure in Pain

Chaos is my pleasure, my ultimate extreme.
I like the pain it gives me or that's how it seems.

I want to feel the love and joy that life is supposed to bring,
But pain is my pleasure, my everything.
When I was growing up, my family was unstable.
I would try to please each and every member, but I was never able.
I needed pain because it felt so right,
To sit and cry my heart out each and every night.

Wishing my mother loved me or my father understood,
Wanting them to notice me like other parents would.
Hoping and praying someday it would be true,
Only to wake each day to fight and argue like we would always do.
Soon I got the message, it became a part of life,
The pain, the turmoil, the grief and strife.

I am now at a loss when things are going good,
Because this is the way I always thought they should.
But because the only pleasure I ever had is pain,
I cannot handle good things, I feel I'm going insane.
I need to learn about real life and the pleasure I can gain,
But because I never knew that life, the pain will remain.
If only life was different and I could go back again,
I would find another pleasure other than in pain.

Excuse Me! 'A drunk driver ran me off the road and I wrecked my mother's car again.'

Stupidest Questions Asked By Students and the Answer
I Didn't Give

Question: I hate to call you at home on Sunday, I have a test tomorrow and can't get my locker open. Can you come to the school?
Answer: Sorry, I can't make it, but I'll have the county search and rescue squad right there.

Question: Uh. . . Mr. Pelanconi. . .Uh. . . I was backing up. . . my rearview mirror isn't, uh. . .Is the brown car in the faculty lot yours?
Answer: No, it's not. I gave it to the French Club demolition derby. Twenty-five cents a swing. One more dent, no big deal.

Question: Can't you just fire Mr. Herkimer? Everybody knows he's a goober.
Answer: The goober will be gone by morning.

Question: Are those four weirdos in the picture behind your desk related to you?
Answer: Those are the Beatles, you idiot. What makes you think your generation invented weirdos?

Question: How do you say 'pizza' in Italian?
Answer: Round Table.

Question: Can we go to Europe on our senior trip?
Answer: Sure.

Question: Is Homecoming a home or away game?
Answer: It used to be home, but we changed it so the other school could clean up the mess.

Question: Can't you remember what it was like being a kid?
Answer: Nope, I was born old.

"How old would you be if you didn't
know how old you are?"
- Satchel Paige

Excuse Me! 'My PE clothes weren't dry and the teacher told me I couldn't miss PE again.'

The Kiosk Was a Good Idea. Students Use It.

TO MY FELLOW FFA MEMBERS AND TO THE DEPT. OF AGRATURE.

Hi iam wrighting this letter i n apoligy. yes it is true that i was caught by two of my x. friends with my dick in a cow milking machine. THE reasons i am apoligising is because iv brought a badname to FFA. again im verry sorry and ill understand if none of you ever talk to me again not that you ever did anyway. iv given it a lott of thought and i hope you all take my letter verry seriously...

sincerly,

FRANKY YUNGER

p.s. i also did something awfull to a sheep.

LOST! AGAIN!! REWARD!!

Jenny Ferguson's virginity in Brickyard Creek. Billy Reynolds is giving a $100.00 Reward to anyone that finds it. She has lost it many times, but if you find it don't tell Billy or he won't give you the Reward.

Excuse Me! 'Mars was in Cancer. I'll be okay now because Jupiter is in Libra.'

An Administrative Delusion

The will to lead; to make the educational train run on time. Not really a lust for power; just a delusion of grandeur that just sort of happened to me. Perhaps it was cultural or even genetic, latent in my Italian immigrant roots. It was the inability to resist being pushed from the vineyards to the winery. It was ego. I thought I knew something.

I became deluded like a pompous Mussolini, who thought it mattered that Italian trains ran on time. The administrative credential was my Ethiopia. Those classes, so irrelevant, were the most boring A's ever endured - yet I mistook the simulation games and scholarly drivel for meaningful educational dogma. I did not see my A's as the possible reflection of my classmates, many of which, in retrospect, had probably blocked one too many punts. I mistakenly thought I was brilliant. A second generation overachiever, I was on my stairway to the bottom.

Looking back, I can't believe I thought I could be a respected member of the community - respected for creative ideas and innovative changes. I actually thought I'd get respect for thinking schools exist for kids and that Sacramento and the unions would agree. I had gotten A's and the profs had written me letters of recommendation. But I should have remembered that I hated golf and didn't even own a pair of those white shoes with nails in the bottom. The Rotary Club did not call and like Orson Wells, I probably wouldn't have joined any organization that would have me as a member.

The realization that the system was immovable from the top was an ugly revelation, perhaps the ultimate Italian joke. However, an early awareness that my notions were folly probably saved me from a Mussolini like fate. I'd made it from the educational vineyard into the winery. Deluded and disgusted, I was getting crazy, which was keeping me from going insane.

To my astonishment, the crazier I got, the better it worked. In many ways the system is so inept that any action is progress. In fact, Postman and Weingartner were right - it actually works best as a subversive activity. So, finally, here I sit in the educational underground (wine cellar?), loving it and even getting a little respect. "Yea, Joe's pretty weird, but people sometimes do the crazy things he throws out there and once in a while they work."

Okay, the train's not on time, but it's running. Lower expectations and subversive activity ain't all bad. I'm content learning that I don't know much. Mussolini should have been the wiser; they strung the poor guy up, didn't they?

"There ain't no rules here. We're trying to get something accomplished."
- Thomas Edison

Excuse Me! 'All of us had head lice, even the dog.'

Hey Wise Guy, What's Your IQ?

Doug

Doug looked rather ordinary. He was a thin, blonde with braces and a shy grin. He was very polite and did little to draw attention to himself. However, it didn't take long to figure out that Doug was special. All you had to do was ask him about most anything. Upon entrance to high school, Doug had scored 800 – the maximum score – on the math portion of the SAT and he hadn't exactly bombed the rest of the test. With this in mind, it didn't take a high SAT score on my part to assume that our school wasn't going to do much for Doug academically. In fact, I told our math department chair to make sure they didn't screw him up. This kid was more than brilliant; he was amazing. His parents were keeping him here for 'maturity and socialization.'

My conversations with Doug were usually about things where I knew far less than he did. This included most everything. He was so knowledgeable on a wide variety of topics and able to converse on most any subject. I think he enjoyed my conversation and maybe I aided his 'maturity and socialization.' However, there were some things there he was just in another zone. Computers were a perfect example, as were talks about MIT, Cal Tech, Stanford and Johns Hopkins. All of these places had called me, since his scores had not gone unnoticed by the best universities in the country. They were asking this C+ grad of Chico State about this kid's academic potential. This in itself defied logic.

Quite unlike Doug, I had resisted computers as long as possible – fervently hoping they'd go away if I ignored them. They didn't and I reluctantly entered virgin territory. I spent one full day and a half during Christmas vacation trying to hook up apples, modems, printers and bytes in my office. I even read the instruction manual twice and could not get the damn thing on line.

Putting ego aside, I called Doug. He came right over. In about 20 minutes he hooked the thing up and had it working. He had also made some corrections in the instruction manual. He politely encouraged me to write the company, since while their instructions were okay, he was sure his revisions would be much easier to understand. I sure as hell didn't doubt him.

I thanked Doug for his help and he courteously assured me that I could learn this computer stuff and that he'd be happy to help me any time. I then gave him several Burger King coupons for his trouble. He lit up, broke into a big smile and enthusiastically blurted, "Hey, that's really cool, thanks!"

Doug entered Stanford at 15. Apparently, we didn't do him any academic harm since he zoomed right through before heading for grad school at UCLA. I'm still not very good with computers.

Excuse Me! 'A computer virus ate my homework. I had to stay home to do it over.'

Principal Thoughts *Bluffer*

Dearest Daughter,

Well, we've made it – you as the principal's daughter and me as the kid's principal. It went so fast, or maybe it's just us old people who think time flies. At any rate, it's over. It's been an experience like any other father and high schooler, yet at the same time, absolutely special.

I can remember the scared 9th grader, afraid she couldn't get her locker open. Sympathetically, I told you to shut up, I'd loan you the master key. And remember you expended a great deal of energy not being seen with me? The way I dressed was oh so embarrassing. Sometimes I was so bad you had to be let out of the car before we got to school. I've still got the same nerdy clothes, but the same threads are now semi-acceptable.

The sophomore year was a treat. You learned to drive – ran the old pickup smack into the oak tree in our front yard. Made me promise not to tell anyone at school. You also gave a speech on how being the principal's kid wasn't so bad, since my office was the biggest locker at school and you had your own instant teller on campus That year you also started dressing like a woman and going to those formals – wobbly heels and all. Quite a shock to the guy who a photo on his desk of you in a softball uniform.

As a junior, I began to get a whole lot smarter. Or at least you began to talk with me as if I was a real person. We even began to argue about things that mattered, like college, apartheid, abortion and if students should be allowed to park in the faculty lot. You finally became the one who was most concerned about learning, grades and stuff like that. Whew! Then there was The Party – one of your very few lapses into total teenage insanity. We lived through it, even talked about it and actually began to view each other as real people.

All of a sudden, you were a senior. You and your friends began to look – even act – like grown people. I feel so lucky that you were in a class that did almost everything right, won all the time and had an amazingly positive attitude. It doesn't even upset me anymore when you politely ignore my advice. I told you that Chico State was the Harvard of our area and that many famous people (me, for example) went there. You chose Humboldt State and, what the heck,it's a good school and green and gold are great school colors.

So my little kid's leaving and I'm still here. I know you and your classmates are going to do very well. I just hope I can do this principal's job without you. I'm going to miss the instant feedback, unsolicited advice, prom dress bills, slumber parties . . . . or am I? It's been great!!

Thanks kid.

Love, Dad

Dearest Dad.

I didn't think I would graduate as the principal's daughter and actually have something nice to say about it. High school has been a positive experience for me, at least I think it has.

On the first day of high school I was like every other freshman. I had the puffy hairsprayed hairdo and tight Guess jeans, rode to school with my dorky dad, but there was one tiny difference. . . my dorky dad was the principal. I was positive he came into all my classes just to spy on me. I dodged him in the hall and if anyone asked, he was a distant cousin by marriage who I hardly even knew.

By sophomore year, I learned that dad didn't spend six years in college to become a principal just to spy on me and see if I cut any classes, but he was still my dad and still kind of a dork. I learned how to make the best out of having my dad always there. I began to talk to him in the hall and learned how to ask for lunch money. THEN I got my license. The big debate began. Can I drive to school? To me it didn't seem logical that dad didn't let me drive to school alone and he share a ride with a neighbor.

Junior year I began to have a few spells, but also began to enjoy having my dad always there, going home and having something in common to talk to my parents about. Maybe dad wasn't that bad. I still got stares and began to get real sick of the question, "How does it feel having your dad as principal?" Then there was The Party . . . Oops, a little spell! But I realized that my dad knew about teen parties and there are a lot worse things he could have been. I was glad he was just the principal.

Now that my senior year is over I know that I was actually very lucky. My dad is not a dork. I now realize my dad is one cool principal. I also know that when I look back on my high school years I'll remember the dances, rallies, but I'll have a memory that only one other person will share . . my dad. Thanks Dad!!!!

Your Loving Daughter

Excuse Me! 'I was absent because my Dad's a dork. You'll have to ask him why he's a dork.'

38

Aw Nesta Gawd This Really Happened

Vandals!

I have come to believe that people's behaviors and attitudes closely reflect their environment. In a fancy restaurant, I can appear very civilized, using a napkin, knife and fork with the best of them. In the grandstand at the Red Bluff Round Up, I can yell and belch with the worst of them. Believing that teenagers are people too, I assume they respond similarly.

Therefore I consider a clean, well groomed and maintained campus a necessity if we expect responsible behavior from teenagers. Fervently advocating this notion, I detest vandalism. It is a passion. Luckily for my blood pressure, it has not been a serious problem at our school - which is sort of my point. To arrive at school and see what some idiot has wrought triggers a helpless, hopeless anger without a release. However, there was this one time.

My wife and I stopped by the school on a Sunday afternoon. I wanted to show her the trees we had just planted. While walking across campus, we heard a loud crash and the sound of breaking glass. It was the large hallway skylight and I could hear the culprits laughing and running across the roof. They were going to jump down and flee.

I beat them to the edge and hid under the eave and, sure enough, two junior high school boys jumped down right in front of me. They froze and I immediately began my verbal litany. They quickly glanced at each other and took off running across the freshly watered lawn. To no avail, I yelled for them to stop. Instinctively, I chased them and surprised myself by catching them both. I must have been saving this dose of adrenaline for years just in case I ever caught a vandal in the act.

I had them both by the arms. They were flailing, scratching, kicking and spitting. The smaller one got away when the big one bit me. I then got him in a bear hug and we wrestled and tussled for what seemed like forever. Finally, we flopped to the ground and began rolling around in the mud. Both of us were too tired to talk, so we just grunted and wriggled around.

Amazingly, I cannot remember questioning the wisdom of a grown man mud wrestling a teen. I do remember the sting of where the snots had bitten me and spitting mud and grass out of my mouth. It just seemed like the thing to do.

I finally got on top of him and began to look for my wife. After what seemed like forever, she came running from the office where she had called the police. I sat on that sucker till the cop arrived, who kept a silly grin on his face the whole time he wrote the report. He kept looking at me, dressed in my muddy Sunday best, still breathing hard and cleaning my scratches and bites. I appreciated his not openly laughing at what was not a typical principal activity. My wife was not so kind.

Excuse Me! 'My uncle tried to kill himself with a bow and arrow.'

MARY R. PANUCCI
District Superintendent

JOSEPH D. PELANCONI
Principal

PAUL GENOUD, Ed.D.
Director, Special Programs

BARGH JOHNSON
Associate Principal

JANICE BLUNCK
Associate Principal

Red Bluff Union High School

(916) 527-7410   (916) 347-3748

1260 Union Street
Red Bluff, California 96080

October 1, 1993

██████████
North Valley Blood Center
285 Cohasset Road
Chico, CA 95926

Dear ████████

I received your letter of September 27 and understand your concern. Red Bluff High School appreciates the possible legal ramifications of an underage donor falsifying information. Rest assured, we will assist you in preventing future occurrences and I have already talked with the guilty donor.

Having said that, let me share my thoughts on the situation. A Red Bluff High student, probably due to peer pressure, sneaked in one day before his legal 17th birthday to donate blood to save a life. I'm sorry, but I find it a great day when our students are feeling pressured to be socially responsible You wrote that he should face "serious disciplinary consequences" for his misdeed. Might I suggest that, as punishment, we extract more blood from him, since he is now legal and that would seem to serve everyone's needs. I do find it commendable that he chose to "come clean." The other three underage donors apparently chose not to confess to your staff.

I also found it interesting that your letter made no mention of the numerous units of blood that apparently survived your scrutiny. Please - allow us to continue to encourage teenagers to donate blood and do keep some perspective. Red Bluff High has a proud tradition of blood donation. How unfortunate that we never communicated until this screw up.

Sincerely,

Joe Pelanconi
Principal

P.S. Just kidding about the three. Lighten up!

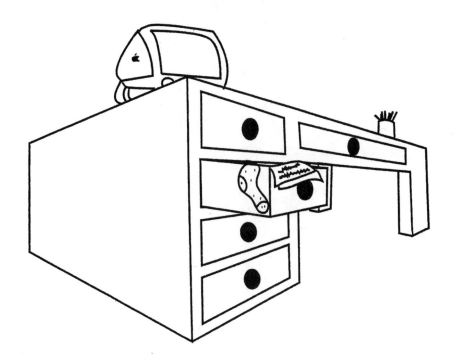

Middle Drawer

During the 80's, Joe tried his best to be a rebel with a cause. This drawer provides living proof that he remained confused and that any meaningful cause completely eluded him.

M.B.

Let Me Whine a Bit

Sure enough, there it was. Right there in the 'Personal' section of the local daily, underneath Sunny's massage therapy ad and right above the SWM looking for same. I usually check the letters to the editor to see if they spell my name right, but the 'Personal' section was a first, I think. One of the secretaries brought it in. "If you have or have had a problem with Mr. Pelanconi write to P.O. Box blah, blah, blah."

Perhaps there's going to be a convention or something; all of the saints who hate my guts in one place at one time to compare notes. They could have breakout sessions on my assaults, abuse charges, lawsuits, personal life rumors, illegal censorship, playing favorites and general rudeness. Tanya Harding could be the keynote speaker. Her talk could be on "How my high school principal screwed me out of Olympic Gold."

The woman from Corning would be there. She's the one who wrote the letter to the editor saying I watched while our students spit on the Corning football players. She could lead a letter to the editor section that would include the guy who writes school 'authorities' illegally censor school plays. The woman who writes that I promote anti-Christian stuff would be there.

The 'playing favorites' session would be crowded. There could be a whole room full of parents who I shafted out of big time athletic and academic scholarship money. The lady who called me a 'Mexican lover' could be in here along with the senora who called me a racist. The facilitator for this bunch would need to be the mother who knows I hate all special ed kids.

If there is a big enough room, the assault, abuse and harassment guys should all meet together. There could be a powerful testimonial from the special ed kid who told the police I made homosexual advances toward him in my office. He could be followed by the kid who was messing around in the lunch line and then charged me with assault when I grabbed him by the jacket. It could go on for days.

The personal life stuff would be the most entertaining and creative. It would be hard to know where to start. My oldest daughter isn't mine? The affair with a teacher? The suicide that was my fault? I'm sure there's a story out there somewhere about me and animals at the farm. This group could invite Geraldo to their session. With his help they'd be on TV. Guaranteed.

The lawsuit group probably should be divided into those who actually sued and those who just threatened to. The threat guys are usually just real angry about something and are just one step up the food chain from the guys who would simply beat the crap out of me. Their group would make a lot of noise, adjourn early and head for the bar.

The guys with actual lawyers would have a long and tedious session. Their group leader would be the guy who sued Bargh and I for a million bucks because we denied his kid his civil rights. The kid burned down a train trestle and told us about it. We called the cops, but the kid got an amnesia attack when the cop arrived. His parents were unavailable. Bargh told him to "cut the bullshit." He did, confessed and was convicted. He didn't win the suit, but the judge did write that Bargh "should not be commended for his use of the term 'cut the bullshit.'" A victory of sorts, I guess.

Now, it is important to note that I've done my share of stupid things and have never claimed to be Mother Teresa. Hey, I'm not whining. Harry Truman was right about that heat and the kitchen stuff. Yet, I really haven't had the time to do all the things I've been accused of, but if a convention would bring some relief to the traumatized, go for it.

It must be the price you pay for being a rich and famous principal.

"Fans don't boo nobodies"

- Reggie Jackson

PERSONALS — 20
ANYONE HAVING or who has had problems with Mr. Pelanconi please write to P.O. Box 220, A-1097, Red Bluff.

Excuse Me! 'Last night his fever was 101, but this morning it's up over 200.'

The Stupidest Questions I Asked Students and the Answers I Got

Question: Did you stop and think before you threw the bark that a custodian would have to clean up your mess?
Answer: No, sir. When I threw the bark I only thought of hitting Frankie in the back of the head.

Question: How did Mike get to the top of the light pole on the football field?
Answer: He climbed right up those ladder things on the side of the pole.

Question: Why in God's name did Mike climb the pole anyway?
Answer: He has family problems.

Question: Is fighting the way your family solves its differences at home?
Answer: Yup.

Question: Don't you think you ought to be in a school where the principal is a whole lot stupider?
Answer: There isn't one.

Question: Why did you pee in Bobby's locker?
Answer: He had it coming.

Question: Isn't it a hassle to spike your blue mohawk every morning?
Answer: Yeah, but it's worth it cause my dad really hates it.

Question: What kind of job do you think you'll get with grades like that?
Answer: A school principal.

"Don't ask me nothin' about nothin'.
I just might tell you the truth."

- Bob Dylan

Excuse Me! 'My dog followed me to school and my first period teacher sent the both of us home.'

This Is What I Thought Then

La Dolce Vita

Three weeks in Italy doesn't make being a principal any easier. Most of what I have on Monday morning's appointment book would warrant, at most, a shrug of the shoulders in Italy. Some items would be amusing and worthy of a hearty Italian laugh, but certainly not the stuff that cultivates ulcers.

Mr. Dimwit wants to see me because students are parking in the faculty lot. Okay. And he's real serious. In Italy, everyone parks everywhere and, yes, it's always confusing and chaotic. Grazia, who we stayed with, parked one night in a neighbor's driveway. He was real agitated and animated the next morning when we arrived at the car. He flagged down a policeman and was ranting on how he missed his 7:00 A. M. appointment. Grazia responded by telling him she had no way of knowing he had an early appointment. The policeman shrugged his shoulders and left and we all drove off. It was over and somehow made sense. Dimwit's going to the staff relations committee if I don't fix this student parking problem within a week. Should I shrug?

There's a lady here wanting to know if the school is going to pay for the cleaning of her expensive dress, since she sat on gum in our performing arts center. Reminds me of the pigeon that shit on Nicki's new leather jacket in Florence. The Italians called it a sign of 'buona fortuna' (good luck) and there were good laughs and a great story. Should I wish this lady 'buona fortuna,' laugh a little at the gum on her butt and escort her out of my office?

There's a kid, sent by his teacher, for cutting the last period of the day. Seems there was a substitute showing a video he'd already seen, so he went home to do his homework. Reminds me of the time I was walking late at night with an Italian friend. On a deserted street corner, I stopped at the red light. He walked across, explaining to me that in Italy those lights are only suggestions. He explained that only an idiot would wait for a light to turn green when there were no cars in sight. Why not compliment this kid on his good sense?

There's a note from the District Office that I won't get paid if I don't get my TB certificate turned in. We flew Alitalia. My wife requested non-smoking seats. Our tickets were marked for smoking. The charming Italian counter man assured us he could quickly get us non-smoking seats. He simply wrote in 'non-smoking' on our tickets and sure enough no one smoked in our seats. Couldn't I sign that TB certificate?

Italians live in a country where there seems to be no rules, nothing seems to be on schedule and no one seems to care. It's no wonder everything appears screwed up and they waste all their time pursuing 'la dolce vita.' Amidst all that chaos and confusion, they just live a lot happier and longer. What fools.

Those dagos are just fools, fools, fools. I've got to keep saying that, so I can do my job. As soon as their life makes perfect sense to me, I'm outa this principal job. I could sell gelato, make vino in a winery, repair Fiats, be an Italian principal . . I could.

Excuse Me! 'Pete had poison oak in special places.'

Feel My Pain

Sensation Addiction

In the overall scheme of world events, high school life is actually rather boring. No teenage scuffle rivals the terrorism of the Middle East, Friday night football games pale in comparison to the Olympics, and no one confuses the breakup of sophomore sweethearts, Twila and Mickey, with the problems of Prince Charles and Di.

Yet, if you were dropped from Mars onto a high school campus and just listened to the chatter, read the notes and witnessed the anguish, you'd summon the United Nations. 9-1-1 would be on everyone's speed dial. There is something built into the teenage psyche that fosters an addictive craving for sensation.

It must have to do with hormones and stuff, since it tends to go away as they approach graduation. Feelings are intense and every event is taken to the emotional extreme. The campus becomes a tragic theater where broken love affairs provide much of the trauma. A fight over 'who said what about her' becomes a major riot when described to Mom and Dad at dinner. These dramas can be very convincing. They often prompt parents to call the principal to find out 'What in the hell's really going on?'

The performances are usually safe and amusing since they have little to do with reality. Teenage needs for tragedy, make Amy's fender bender the outlet for extended wailing. Rumor enhancement provides crippling injuries, brutal cops, unsympathetic principals and parents who 'just don't understand.' It's all the theater they can handle - and Amy's just fine. They play 'tragedy' like preschoolers play 'house.'

When just feeding the sensation addiction, teens know that reality is far removed. There are no consequences or actual loss. Twila can make a miraculous recovery from a broken heart. The notion of real trauma, like death, pushes teens into a perplexity beyond comprehension. It's a way-out-there zone that allows a bit of reality to feed the sensation addiction. Their ability to quickly rebound from the virtual tragedies, suggests that actual reality is a confusing concept for them.

The death of a teen, even one who no one knows, can paralyze them in large numbers. They have a keen awareness that death is a big deal and no one will dare tell them to knock off the mourning. My 14 year old daughter's softball team once couldn't take the field because a senior boy had been killed. They were in the dugout hugging and sobbing uncontrollably, while the other team kept warming up. Coaches and parents were powerless. None of the players had ever met the deceased.

They recovered after twenty minutes and played the game. Luckily, Polly got injured - again. It was the fifth time that season. This time it was an ankle. Teammates had to carry her off the field, run for ice and help her through a tough two innings in the dugout. They won the game in their last at bat, and Polly miraculously joined them at home plate for the high five celebration. I asked my daughter if she knew the dead boy. His name was Mike Somebody and Polly might need x-rays. Such is the emotional life of teens. Teen life may be boring, but what you hear from them sure makes up for it.

Excuse Me!   'He misses school because he's thinking with his penis.'

47

Aw Nesta Gawd This Really Happened

Arquimedes

Tom was one of the top scholars in the senior class. He was a quiet, polite and popular kid headed for UC Berkeley. He was also Hispanic, with English as his second language.

Not surprisingly, Tom was selected to give a graduation speech. I had no doubt that he could write and deliver a dynamite speech. The kid was a winner. I called him in to discuss his topic and ask how he wanted his name in the program.

I started with the simple program stuff.   "Do you want it to say 'Tom'?" "No." "'Thomas'?" "No" "'Tomas'?" "No." Confused and a bit embarrassed, I asked, "What is your name? I've never heard anyone call you anything but Tom." "You've never met my family," he replied. "My name is Arquimedes."

"Arkywhat? Why do we call you Tom?" He then explained to me that neither he nor his parents spoke any English when he enrolled in kindergarten. The teacher couldn't handle Arquimedes, so she called him Tom. That's been his "school name" ever since.

He explained that many in his family are limited English speakers and he'd like them to recognize his name in the program even if they couldn't understand all of his speech. That got us to thinking. His was not the only Hispanic family who might have difficulty understanding.

Why not give his speech in Spanish? So he did. It was well received by the largely Anglo, and rather surprised, crowd. I understood quite a bit of it, although one of our Spanish teachers told me he said something about my mother. I don't think that's true. Arquimedes was too nice a kid. He should have said something about his kindergarten teacher, though.

"Being fair is not treating everyone the same. Being fair is treating everyone how he needs to be treated."

- Mickey Bitsko

Excuse Me! 'My pet rat bit my lip.'

Aw Nesta Gawd This Really Happened

Butch's Hog

I can't believe I bought Butch's hog at the Junior Livestock Auction. Not only did I bid on and buy the thing, but I paid a premium price for a pig that looked just like all the rest of them and was raised by public enemy number one.

Old Butch didn't slide into high school unnoticed; he'd punched out a kid at freshman orientation. With red flags all over him, he'd gone directly to the Opportunity program. Known for chewing, spitting and fighting, Butch had been accused of all kinds of assaults. He usually admitted his part and took the suspensions in stride, as sort of a cost of doing business. His fights were usually the result of his meting out a justice that only he fully understood. It generally had to do with some cowchick's or close friend's honor.

Butch came from a cowboy family that doesn't exactly embrace education. Some would say they haven't warmed up to civilization much either. They are known for driving real ugly pick-up trucks, talking real slow and punching real fast. Most have endured high school until they could get what they thought was a good paying job. Teaching school isn't on their list, but lazy they aren't.

Now, not everyone at school dislikes Butch. Some would even say, old Butch never punched anyone who didn't have it coming. The ag teachers are rather fond of him. He is a hard worker, does more than his share at the school farm and adds a new dimension to security at F.F.A. fund raising events. I have always gotten along with him, even through several suspensions. He has always been very respectful, painfully honest, and I have no intention of bad mouthing his friends.

Butch isn't the best-looking creature you've ever seen and neither was his hog. Yet, I've got the photo of both of them hanging in my office. The hog looks well groomed and attentive; Butch, without his black cowboy hat and short hair, worn clothes, sour look and chewing tobacco fat lip, looks rather bored. People see that picture and can't believe the principal of the school bought Butch's hog.

I can't believe it either, but I have to tell you that this expensive pork is the best I've ever tasted.

"If slaughterhouses had glass walls, everyone would be a vegetarian."
- Paul McCartney

Excuse Me! 'I butted heads with my horse. My horse is okay.'

Principal Thoughts *Bluffer*

Mr. Anonymous

A high school principal gets lots of advice. Nearly everyone went to high school, so most people have some definite ideas on how it should work. Generally, I look forward to hearing what people have to say. Most are truly interested in sharing ideas, understanding the school and discussing ways we can improve. Listening, responding and changing are important parts of my job. After all, it is a public school and we're not perfect.

However, there is one guy out there that wastes both his time and mine. His name is Mr. (Ms.?) Anonymous. He sometimes calls; other times he writes. Sometimes the suggestions make sense, other times they are just cheap shots about my mother and things. He has to be among the homeless, since he never gives a return address or phone number. I looked up Anonymous (first name of Alcoholics) in the phone book, but it was not the guy I wanted.

Mr. Anonymous is an interesting dude and is an expert on teenage dress, music and an authority on nearly everything. He usually sends a clear directive for the principal to change something immediately to meet his standards. Something like "you should have a rule and ban those Raider jackets (or substitute cowboy hats)."

A particular area of expertise is athletics, with advice for coaches a specialty. However, he often seems to get confused. Sometimes he is critical because we don't win enough; other times we win too much at the expense of all kids not playing. I'd love to discuss our athletic (or performing arts,

ag, etc.) policies and philosophy with him, but with no phone and living in a cardboard box somewhere, I don't know how to find him.

Now, it has occurred to me that maybe Anonymous is a phony name - just a made up moniker for someone too weird or insecure to discuss an issue eyeball to eyeball. Hey, nobody's too weird. I work real hard to listen to students, staff, parents and community members and treat them all with dignity and respect. It's their school - even the weird ones.

Or maybe old Anonymous had a real hard time in school and doesn't feel comfortable talking with principals. The awful grammar and spelling of most of the notes supports this theory. That's too bad, because some of his ideas are worth discussing and I can be rather reasonable, even friendly. He needs to feel good about school.

But if he's too spooked of me, I would suggest he go to the source of his concern. In most cases, it's best to talk to those closest to the situation anyway. In all probability, the football coach can explain better than me why Weezer Alderberry doesn't play defensive tackle. Maybe someday I'll get a chance to tell him this simple truth.

But until this character comes out of the closet, I'll politely listen to the calls and toss the notes into the round Mr. Anonymous file. It's sad that I have to waste time on this gutless wonder, because I think he really does care, could definitely benefit from additional information and perhaps help us be a better and more responsive school. Besides, I'm dying to meet this guy. Anybody out there know him?

"Never answer an anonymous letter."
- Yogi Berra

Excuse Me! 'My SAT score depressed me big time. I couldn't get up.'

Mrs. Evans,

I'm really sorry for putting a condom in your coffe cup. Because I knew it really embarrased you. I know what I did was very stupid, childish, and disrespectful.

The reason I did it was because I got dared to do it, and I took the dare. Even though I knew it would get me in trouble, I did it anyways. I thought I wouldn't get caught, but I felt guilty and that's why I was honest.

I'm very sorry and I won't do nothing stupid like that again.

Arturo

Rambling Thoughts at a Teen Funeral

Alfred, Suicide and What's Fair

A series of recent events got me to thinking - a meeting with parents of the "gifted," a funeral and report card time. As we haggle over higher expectations, weighted grades for honors classes and the athletic code, the question of 'what's fair?' keeps coming up.

You know the questions:

Is it fair to grade our elite on a five point scale?

Is it fair to have an elite?

Is it fair to grade anyone?

Is it fair to have different standards for the less capable?

To me, the questions are baffling, not to mention the answers. However, it does remind me of the time in 5th grade when Alfred and I got caught cheating. I grew up in the wine country. Back then, your family either owned the fruit or picked the fruit. My family wasn't wealthy, but my father and uncles either owned ranches or worked in wineries. Alfred was one of twelve kids whose families picked the fruit. More specifically, Mom and the kids picked grapes and Dad drank wine.

Socially, Alfred was a misfit at best. Academically, Alfred was a quart low, which is what we said back before someone invented special ed. We were both in 5th grade, even though he had a beard and hair under his arms. Somehow we got caught cheating. I was giving him the answers. He surely wasn't giving them to me and this was way before they invented cooperative learning. Yes, I cheated, but it just wasn't fair. The teacher called my parents, while his weren't available.

She lowered my grade; Alfred's was already as low as it could go. I couldn't play in the basketball game; he hadn't made the team. My parents were crushed and "so disappointed;" his probably never knew. To me, it just wasn't fair. I hated that teacher. It looked to me like Alfred pretty much got off and I got crucified.

Looking back, it really wasn't fair. The teacher should have done more to me. Alfred had gotten in the wrong line when they handed out parents, brains and most everything else. It hadn't been fair since we were born. It also isn't fair that I've got umpteen college units and there's a 15 year-old in this school who is ten times smarter than me.

At the funeral the other day, I was thinking that too many teen traumas and more than a few teen suicides also aren't fair. Somebody else's expectations all too often program the outcome. How sad that well-meaning people are imposing their expectations, just trying to be fair. This poor victim had people around him who had no big picture; no realization that raising and teaching kids is not an exact science. Kids are different. Not all were meant to follow dad to medical school. Kids don't come with an owner's manual. Parenting and teaching are art forms.

So this leads me to the sloppy and easily debatable conclusion that we simply must portray an illusion of fairness. Every youngster needs to feel he is treated fairly, even though he maybe treated differently. This is where my 5th grade teacher was clueless. Her intuitions were right on. I would have accepted it and never hated her if she had given me the illusion that Alfred had also gotten his. Great teachers do that sort of thing routinely. They know that one youngster needs a kick in the pants while another a pat on the back in identical situations. Ironically, these teachers are usually perceived as being very fair.

In *Prince of Tides,* there's this one sequence, where the narrator, Tom, beats up the rich and nasty Newbury kid. The principal, fearing for his job, agrees to severely discipline Tom. The conversation between Tom and the principal reads:

"If you ever get into a fight in my school again, Tom, I'm going to take the skin off your ass, and that's a promise. And if you ever fight Todd Newbury again and don't do a better job of shutting his mouth, I'm going to whip you within an inch of your life. Do you understand me?"

"Yes sir," I said.

"Now, I'm going to hit the paddle on this geography book. Every time I do, you give out a yelp. Make it convincing. Because I'm going to tell Reese Newbury that I tore your butt up." He struck the book hard with his paddle and I yelled. It was in Mr. Roe's office that I decided to become a teacher.

Without this art form, all of our yapping about fairness is just plain baloney. Forget the rule; do the right thing. Interestingly, Tom, like most kids, immediately understood how the world works. My 5th grade teacher was no Mr. Roe.

Higher expectations, absent Mr. Roe's insight, simply betray the bright ones and frustrate the rest. I have no need to shoulder the guilt for teen misery and suicide, I have an obligation to not add to the problem. I shudder when I hear teachers talk about grading on the curve or rigid codes of conduct rigidly applicable in all situations. Hasn't anyone else met Alfred or been to a teen funeral?

Life's not fair. If Alfred hadn't died in a motorcycle crash, I'd have him tell you. If this kid hadn't committed suicide, I'd have him tell you.

"Do the right thing. It will gratify some people and astonish the rest."
- Mark Twain

Excuse Me! 'It all started when my father found out he was adopted.'

53

Staying Sane at Meetings

Bored Zone

School Boards are an institution that I really never could figure out. I know they have to do with democracy, public input, checks and balances and all that, but it often just doesn't seem to make much sense. Basically, you pick five people off the street who went to some school and have them set policy for a rather complex and complicated system. Seems to me, Boards spend most of their time learning about educational systems, listening to public gripes and firing and hiring a superintendent now and then. Mark Twain may have been a bit harsh when he compared board member to monkeys, but it is food for thought.

In twenty something years I have been to probably three hundred something school board meetings. That's probably about a thousand and something hours listening to stuff that, well, just isn't very exciting. In fact, I have been very lucky to have nearly all of them be boring board meetings. Exciting board meetings usually mean a hostile audience and are much worse than boring ones. Trust me on that one.

Nearly all of the dozens of board members I've known have been decent, sincere people wanting to do what's right for schools, even though they knew precious little about how schools operate. They got paid nothing, took all kinds of abuse, yet they generally worked hard to defend public education. You've got to be a good person to do that. It probably also means you are not very zany or entertaining. A few have been idiots and even fewer have been zealots with a personal agenda and, as I'll mention later, these few do serve a purpose.

For the first few meetings way back when, I tried to pay attention, hang on every word and figure out what was going on. It was real hard. They'd be discussing whether or not students wearing sandals was a health and safety or dress code issue, while my brain kept jumping to summers in Baja where everyone on the beach is barefoot. When someone asked me something, my mind had to instantly jump miles and focus on something much less interesting than San Felipe. I would stutter and stammer and everyone knew I was daydreaming. It was nerve wracking.

Then I discovered the Bored Zone. The idea came from a visit to Alcatraz. I became interested in the Birdman of Alcatraz. As a lifer in solitary, the Birdman had found a way to shrink his world, zero in on birds and pass, even enjoy, his time. I, too, was imprisoned in solitary and threatened with excruciating boredom. I needed to find a way to become engrossed with something right in front of me, so that the jump back to reality could be quick and undetected. Enter the Bored Zone.

Most board meetings were at night and the windows were closed, so birds were out of the question. I considered insects, but they were not dependable. What I came up with was a series of activities that I could quickly move into depending on the situation. All were designed to be right in front of me, tolerant of quick interruption, and would allow me to respond with something besides a 'duh' or 'huh' when called upon. It was the Bored Zone - a semi-trance state that kept you lucid and occupied, yet amply sedated.

Candy was always the first choice. More than one board member had a habit of bringing hard candy to meetings. The best was Al the Candyman. Al always had interesting candy that he slipped out of his briefcase and over to me right after 'approval of the minutes.' You can time how long it takes to totally dissolve a lemon drop without biting it, which you can do in 4:51 if you use your tongue a lot. Slowly savoring the candy can take several agenda items. Folding the candy wrapper into origami type things can take you all the way to the 'budget report.'.

Another favorite has been the student members of the board. For some reason, they have always seemed to share my Birdman instincts. Perhaps it's a maturity thing. Casey was the best. She even brought small foam rubber puzzles to the meetings. We would each have one and race to see who could put theirs together first, all the while appearing to be interested in every agenda item. The puzzles were not easy and they often took four or even five agenda items. Casey was good and usually beat me. It irritated me that she could do it while looking more interested in the meeting than I.

There were also note passers. For many years I sat at the table next to Dennis, the curriculum coordinator. He was the best. As an English teacher, Dennis could slip me caustic and well written observations as well as pointed, and often humorous, questions. He had such a serene and sincere smile that he could do this totally undetected. I was not as subtle and usually smirked or made weird faces after reading his stuff. I always thought the board should know the real Dennis, but I never exposed him. After all, he could keep me in the Zone.

The absolute best Bored Zone technique, however, was and is doodling. I recommend it for anyone. Twenty something years ago, I had no artistic talent and years later I still have none. However, I have moved from simple blue ball point circles and squares to multi-colored fine point felt tip pen masterpieces. The beauty of doodling is that others think you're taking notes, when you're really drawing the '41 Buick you drove in high school - in five different colors.

I have produced some very extensive doodling works, and much of it was done right on the agenda itself with no one being the wiser - except maybe Dennis, who is an excellent doodler in his own right. Some of the masterpieces actually express my true feelings about board meetings. Luckily, I have not shared these with anyone, but, trust me, they are classics. The Birdman would understand and appreciate the effort.

Now, as for the members with diminished brain capacity and/or misguided missions, they must have been the ones who prompted Mark Twain's quip. Every Board must have at least one who can interrupt boredom with the stupidest of comments. Sadly, in this time of heightened school accountability, these dolts must be taken seriously by someone, especially superintendents who give a rip about job security. Not me, though; they're just momentary breaks from Baja.

There's the ludicrous, like the time during real tight money times, that we spent $5,000 for new wood on the baseball bleachers. A Board member had gotten a sliver in her butt at a Little League game and angrily livened up the next meeting with the lurid details. She was hard enough to keep happy without a pain in her rear, so the maintenance guys flew into high gear.

One, in particular, was rude beyond belief. An impeccably dressed professional, he must have imagined that election to the board was a precursor to a budding political career. His boredom at meetings obviously far exceeded mine, and he did nothing to conceal it. Meeting in the school library, he often pulled books off shelves and thumbed through them during agenda items he deemed insignificant. Once after a student presentation, several students commented to me that such rudeness would not be allowed in any classroom on campus.

Then there's the single-issue zealots, like the guy who fervently believed schools were about athletics and not much else. He'd doze through curriculum and budget presentations, but come unglued if he wasn't informed about the new volunteer doing yard markers at football games. He once threw a mini tantrum when he was 'shocked' to know we'd changed the color of the softball uniforms without Board input.

There are also the ones who are just plain fools. They'd be embarrassing, at best, if there was ever was an outside observer in the audience who didn't know that these folks are just the price we pay for democracy. Like the time we had a biology teacher make a presentation on the need for a new Advanced Placement biology textbook. He had researched AP and college courses and reviewed every available high school text. The whole sicence department and the School Site Council had reviewed texts. He was proposing adopting a text more in line with the AP exam. One Board member proudly announced she must vote 'No' on the text because it mentions evolution, which she said she didn't believe in. The student member of the Board pointed out that Darwin and his theories existed and, in fact, are a part of the exam. The 'No' vote was undaunted. I wanted to note that I didn't believe in slavery, but supported having history texts that mentioned it.

As a veteran doodler, I was silent on the evolution issue. Luckily I'd learned that one must just smile at times like this and be grateful for something that interrupted the doodling. I did, however, wonder if this was in any way connected to Mark Twain's remark about monkeys and Board members.

"God made monkeys; that was just for practice. Then he made school boards."

- Mark Twain

Excuse Me! 'Stormy was under the weather.'

Noise That Annoys

Garage Rock

Every high school has to have at least one garage rock band. It is a rule, I think. The group always has a drummer and several guitarists. These are mandatory. Once in awhile they'll throw in a lead singer, who might double as a tambourine aficionado. Sometimes there's a guy with a saxophone, keyboard or something like that.

The noise they make is always deafening. The sound is awful. While I am no music critic, the quality always ranges somewhere between 'fingernails on the blackboard' and 'agonizing pain.' I have always wanted to ask if they are maybe playing different tunes, but I'm pretty sure they think they're groovin' together.

A quick glimpse at their instruments helps one understand why they may not have a tight sound. At least one of the guitarists has a broken guitar string flying around. I think this is an important touch, since it is proof that they are serious and play real hard. The drummer always (and I mean *always*) has adhesive tape on his drum head. This does not prevent him from doing the mandatory drum solo.

Appearances are everything to these guys. They may not be able to sound like stars, but they can almost look like them. They dress in tie-dye, grunge or whatever else they've just seen a lot of on MTV. Hair is real important and bandanas can add a special touch. They shake their heads furiously to get the hair flying. That is important, but I think their sound might be better served if they took a peek or two at what part of the guitar they were strumming.

They do not lack for energy, often jumping and flailing all over the place. Most groups try to work some sexually explicit gyrations into their act, since that seems to add a touch of credibility. Since the lyrics are impossible to decipher, they have to do something visual to be a bit offensive. The real brazen groups try the Michael Jackson crotch grab. That will usually get the attention of everyone, including the principal.

It is important to look like you are into the music. Closing one's eyes with your headway back is good, as is looking at your feet with your hair over your face. Either of these moves coupled with body jerks that roughly correspond to what the drummer is doing is really cool. Some have the added ability to appear to be on drugs. That calls for a special spaced out, glazed look that only the best groups can pull off.

The name of the group is critical and can also address the credibility issue. Names like 'PMS' or 'Dying Salamanders' look real good on posters.   My favorite group name was 'The Dick Nixons.' It sort of had a disrespectful, counterculture ring to it and did not entirely ignore the sexual innuendo requirement. Unfortunately, I could not tell 'The Dick Nixons' sound from any of the other groups.

Finding a difference among groups is not easy for me. We had a group who said they had a 'country influence.' They were called 'Roadkill.' They had a grubby Willie Nelson look about them, but I swear they sounded just the same as 'PMS' to me.

Not only is it difficult to tell the groups apart, it is impossible to tell one song from another. In fact, I have never been able to tell when they quit warming up and start playing for real. I am always particularly amused when after playing a twenty minute 'set,' the lead whatever goes to the mike and announces that they will now play an original song they wrote. They begin and, honesta gawd, it sounds just like all the rest of them.

Their parents tell me they practice a lot and that their neighbors often threaten to organize, but not as anything resembling a fan club. They spend a lot of money on equipment, blow electrical fuses, and frighten household pets. Hey, but they could be out stealing hubcaps and, who knows, maybe there's a rock star in the garage.

It is a different story at school. These groups play their 'music' at rallies or lunch time activity type things. They have great followings with their loyal fans clapping and swaying to the noise. Their songs end to ovations, screams and cheers. Freshmen girls, especially, are enthralled by the event and mesmerized by the artists. It is kind of a 'put it in your mother's face' experience for them. The mandatory drum solo brings the loudest raves.

Don't get me wrong. It's great that youngsters express themselves through music, and I suppose all of today's rock stars started out in someone's garage. The Beatles did that, didn't they? But let's return to a saner time. Today's teens are too weird. In my day, the 60's, rock music was innocent and lyrical. Talent and tact prevailed. In fact, our vice principals seem to be relatively normal folks and one of them was the lead in a group called 'Ruptured Richard and the Crudeouts.' Those were the days.

An Anonymous Note on My Desk

Mr. P.,

This school is to damn hard.
What do you think, we are interletuals
or something?

Excuse Me! 'My parents will be home today. I had to clean up the house after the party.'

Principal Thoughts *Bluffer*

Go Radishes!

Have you heard all the flap about the Atlanta BRAVES? It seems that some American Indians are upset and find that mascot and the tomahawk chop degrading. No one can deny that Native Americans have been treated unfairly and are certainly deserving of our dignity and respect.

However, the Braves are not exactly a new item. The Boston Braves baseball team was founded in the l890's, later moved to Milwaukee and finally to Atlanta . Why is this issue surfacing now? Obviously, people must be getting more sensitive.

Perhaps we can look forward to Catholics protesting the San Diego PADRES and their silly little bald-headed monk mascot. Or how about Scandanavian Americans getting after the Minnesota VIKINGS and those dumb looking horns they have painted on their helmets? Maybe its a matter of time until some buckaroos somewhere get fired up about the Dallas COWBOYS?

All of which leads me to the SPARTANS. Red Bluff High must have had an election a long time ago and chose the Spartan as our mascot. Maybe it was just blind luck that we are not called the Red Bluff Rednecks. Spartans, of course, were bloodthirsty and courageous warriors of ancient Greece. Could our use of spartan be offending some Greek Americans?

In an attempt to answer this question, I asked two Red Bluff High students of Greek heritage. This is what they told me. John Vlahakis said "I'm proud of my Greek heritage, Spartans is fine with me." Nick Vovakes stated

"They were valiant fighters and I'm not at all offended by the use of Spartans as a mascot."

From this I can conclude that while we must be sensitive to the feelings of various groups, at this time Spartans does not appear to be a problem. But who knows what lurks ahead? If the Braves become the Atlanta Apples due to some strong pressure, the whole idea of mascots may need to be rethought.

It would be easy to say that ethnic or other groups of people are out - no Celtics, Warriors, Redskins, Fighting Irish, 49ers, whatever. Everyone must go with an animal. Not so fast. Can you imagine if they had innocently voted us the Red Bluff Spotted Owls? Do you think Spotted Owls would fly as a mascot in Tehama County? Chainsaws would replace the Brave tomahawks. Whoa!

Sometimes I think we all take ourselves a bit too seriously. Maybe being a principal thickens your skin, but the Red Bluff Romans sounds fine to this Italian American. My parents always taught me to be proud of what I was, regardless of the facts. I also find it amusing that the Cherokee Indians are making big money selling fake tomahawks to Braves fans and find the mascot quite acceptable.

It seems to me that no professional team or school ever intended to mock any particular group. Nonetheless, we may see the day when everybody's a vegetable. That might work. I can see it now - the Red Bluff Radishes smash the Anderson Artichokes!

However, for now I agree with John and Nick. Let's stick with the SPARTANS.

"Too many folks don't take humor seriously."
- Mickey Bitsko

Excuse Me! 'I thought it was Saturday.'

Aw Nesta Gawd This Really Happened

High on Oregano

It all started a while back, so the details are a bit fuzzy. I remember that Bob was the new VP and he had cleverly engineered his first drug bust. He had the teary eyed suspect seated in his office. The full baggie of marijuana was on Bob's desk, sitting there like a trophy of sorts. Bob called the police and then left his office to get me and share the prize. When we returned to his office, the kid was there, but the marijuana was nowhere in sight. Bob frantically looked on the floor, under the chair and then searched the kid. No dope. Bob was getting nervous and I was getting amused.

We put the kid in another office and questioned the secretaries to see if they had noticed anything. There were no leads and no marijuana. We decided it had to be in Bob's office somewhere. Sure enough, we found it stuffed into a book shelf right behind the Ed Code. The cop arrived about the time we got our act together. I found this sequence funnier than it probably really was. We called Bob Super Slueth, Sherlock and other not-so-kind things. I went to the faculty break room and made sure everyone else would taunt him. It was the least I could do; he'd do the same for me.

The next morning I got to my office early and right under my daily planner was this baggie stuffed with a leafy green substance. I looked around to see who was watching and then opened the baggie. My big nose and Italian heritage told me it was pure oregano. You had to love Bob's sense of humor. I put the baggie in my bottom desk drawer. All that week I found more oregano baggies, in my file cabinet, behind books and in drawers. I slipped them all into that bottom drawer.

Over the next year or so, the oregano baggies were rather handy. Whenever I found a kid who reeked of marijuana, was zonked and lying, I'd just reach into that drawer and throw a baggie at his feet. "Look what you dropped. I thought you were just a user, didn't know that you were a big time dealer." It worked every time. It was like an injection of truth serum. "Holy shit, man, I smoked some weed, yea, but that dope ain't mine!" "You're right," I'd say. "Now let's talk about your smoking dope during school time." The oregano went back into the drawer with the rest of my stash.

It stayed there till the other night, when some pothead broke into the office and vandalized the place. He made a real mess, but no one could find anything missing - except me and I wasn't talking. All of my desk drawers were dumped and my oregano was gone. Do you think he'd once seen something leafy come out of those drawers?

The police caught the kid the same night breaking into a neighboring house. The newspaper said he was cited for a bunch of things including possession of "baggies containing a green, leafy substance suspected to be marijuana." Hmm.

Sorry, but I'm not admitting to anything. But I would have loved to have seen the officer's face if the kid said he stole the dope from the principal. Okay, I'll admit to being an oregano user, but I'm no big time dealer.

Excuse Me! 'One of Mom's boyfriends died. I went to the funeral.'

All In a Day's Mail. . .

A letter from a guy in prison who thinks his son attends our school (he has really moved). He writes much more than I want to know about the bum rap that got him into prison and how much he loves Junior, even though "I haven't been much of a father from the inside." He begs me to deliver the enclosed letter to Junior. That letter tells Junior the same stuff that was in my letter, but has interesting twist. It seems Dad is going to the parole board and maybe Junior could rethink "how it all came down," since he was "real young and badly influenced by his mother" when the cops talked to him. Junior could please write and just maybe help out and then old Dad could get back to being super father, just like it was before the bum rap.

A resume from a guy in Venice Beach who wants a teaching job. He has never taught school, but has worked two years as a therapist for "sexually dysfunctional couples." He followed that with a year as a troubleshooter for Goldfinger Enterprises and is currently the marketing director for Infinity Films. Now this may reveal some of my weird prejudices, but I've been to Venice Beach. I've seen the therapists and troubleshooters on the beach and skating down the boardwalk. The film places appear interesting. I'm not sure that this guy'd be able to smoothly slide right into the Red Bluff faculty room.

A letter from Jared, a kid who had graduated and then came back to vandalize the school. He's real sorry for the mess he made.

A Jack-in-the Box coupon for a free hamburger after their tainted meat scandal had killed a kid and made a bunch of others ill. No note, nothing, just the coupon. Is this a death threat?

A letter from the State Department about a Sacramento meeting where "our office will be distributing numerous documents. Because of the large volume of materials, you may wish to bring containers, boxes, or bags, that will make it easier for you to take these materials back to your district." How nice.

A note from a neighborhood landlord who lost his best tenant, an 86-year-old lady, because the elderly renter discovered two high school kids having sex in her carport. Could I do something so he doesn't lose any more tenants?

A letter from Marco, the owner of Marco's American Hotdogs, wanting to know if he could set up a hotdog stand at the graduation ceremony.

A letter from a mother who wants her money back for her son's yearbook because his friends wrote "disgusting things" in it while he was at school.

A letter from a guy working on his doctoral dissertation at the University of Southern California. He is researching what principals believe to be the most "irrelevant and time consuming distractions" of their job. He assures me that his survey will only take about an hour of my time to complete.

Excuse Me! 'It was the Grand Opening at Wal-Mart.'

Aw Nesta Gawd This Really Happened

Kyle

Finding the humor or irony in most of what happens at school is my way of keeping a smirk on my face and the Tums in the drawer. After all, better people than me have decided that being a high school principal ain't much fun. Some call me callous, clueless or both, but I like to think of myself as a survivor. For me, it works - most of the time.

When Kyle died, it did not work. There was no humor, irony, sense or nonsense in what happened. A seventeen-year-old junior, he was with the track team at a dual meet when he somehow bounced off the pole vault pad and struck his head. They disconnected the life support system several days after the accident.

Kyle was a good kid - one that anyone would want for a son. He was personable, good looking, a decent student, had a sense of humor, lived all his life in Red Bluff. He had a mom, dad, brother, sister, girlfriend, buddies, a future. His track coaches loved him. He didn't do anything wrong.

The track meet was at Shasta College, the best facility around. The weather was perfect. The event was supervised by the college vaulting coach. The first aid was by the book and perfect. The paramedics were there in two minutes, the ambulance in ten, Mercy Hospital in fifteen.

As principal, you spend a lot of time assuring teenagers that good things happen to people who do the right thing. Go to class, get involved in sports, follow the rules, have a positive attitude and you'll be fine. Kyle died when he was seventeen years old and there was no lesson to be taught and certainly not any humor.

What does a big shot principal tell Kyle's friends, big, full grown boys with tears running down their cheeks? "Mr. Pelanconi, he wasn't drinking or driving crazy, why?" "Since kindergarten we were the three musketeers, now Kyle's gone, we don't understand."

Neither do I.

> *"I wish I had the answer to that,*
> *because I'm tired of answering*
> *that question."*
> *- Yogi Berra*

Excuse Me! 'We had an appointment with our lawyer. We are going to sue the school.'

You Gotta Like This Guy

Maurice

There is one kid at our school who has gotten at least as much action out of the administration as the teachers' union or the Board of Trustees. His name is Maurice, although I don't really know him and don't think I've ever seen the guy.

He's my e-mail buddy, creating both entertainment and action. About a year ago, Maurice sent me an e-mail complaining that some vandals were letting the air out of his bike tires while parked in the bike rack near the library. He thought the principal should know and if he had any "sense of justice," he'd do something.

I e-mailed him back, telling him to quit whining. It would be much more "adult" if he would propose a solution. He did. Maurice suggested a video camera mounted on the library roof, with a monitor on the librarian's desk, where the librarian "can always be found staring straight ahead at nothing in particular." According to him, the camera would identify the culprits and give the librarian a meaningful role at the school.

"Bad idea," I e-mailed him back. The camera scheme would be too expensive and the librarian actually had other things to do, despite his observations. I suggested he come up with a proposal of lesser cost. He did. Maurice then suggested that we tie his neighbor's dog to the bike rack, since it would bark at anything that moved, providing an excellent alarm system at low cost. He'd donate the dog food. The librarian could then just walk to the window when the mutt barked and identify the tire flattener.

I actually considered this idea, but e-mailed Maurice that I had an even better idea. He should just bring his bike to my office and he could park it next to my desk during the school day. Since I spent most of my day at my desk reading and writing Maurice e-mails, I could easily watch for a bad guy trying to mess up his bike. He must have thought it was a stupid idea, since he quit sending e-mails.

I must confess that every day after that I went by the library bike rack while out on campus. Sometimes I spotted a kid and always wondered if it was Maurice or maybe a vandal. I never considered seeking him out, but did tell one of the vice principals and the librarian to keep their eyes open for bike rack trouble.

Yesterday, almost a year later, Maurice was back on my screen. This time, he he feels cheated by an "out of control bureaucracy." It seems Maurice broke his leg last year (which may explain why he gave up on the bike rack issue) and missed a lot of his P.E. class. He says he had a doctor's note, turned it in and the bureaucracy proceeded to dock him a credit of P.E. "Grossly unfair," he says. "Is there any justice?," he asks. At my suggestion, his counselor was checking into it within minutes. Maurice got an instant e-mail reply from me, assuring him that the bureaucrats were getting right on it. I loved hearing from him. I'll get to my appointments sooner or later. Right now, we've got to take care of Maurice.

There can't be many Maurices. It will be great hearing his name called and handing the e-mail mystery man his diploma. Or maybe I'll just e-mail it to him

Excuse Me! 'My mother had a hurt feeling in her knee.'

63

Aw Nesta Gawd This Really Happened

Horse Sense

You've got to like the cowboy kids. Sitting on the tailgates of their pickup trucks, listening to country music, they harken back to a simpler time. Decked out in boots, Wranglers, with either oversized cowboy hats or Alber's Feed baseball caps, they preserve and protect a threatened ridin' and ropin' value system. All this, and most don't even know a horse, let alone ride one.

They hang out at what they call 'cowboy corner,' a table and coke machine in the pickup truck section of the student parking lot. They can be a bit rowdy at times, but are usually quite respectful of adults and young girls in tight Wranglers. Their "live and let live" philosophy is probably more about rugged individualism than tolerance, but it works. Consequently, it was a surprise to me when I heard what they did at lunch yesterday. It seems that a rather special freshman named Frankie was doing his usual annoyances to attract their attention. Someone suggested Frankie take off his pants and run around the flagpole. Another suggested that there'd be big money in such a stunt.

Before long, there was a cowboy hat on the table, with guys throwing in dollar bills. Butch counted them and announced there was $52 in the hat. In a flash, Frankie took off his boots and pants and streaked for the flagpole, about 100 yards away. The cheering rivaled any good bull ride at the Red Bluff Roundup.

However, before an exhausted Frankie returned, the guys had grabbed their dollars out of the hat. The bell then rang, and they all headed for class. A teacher had heard the commotion and was headed for cowboy corner. He gave me some names and a rough sketch of what had happened. Almost instantly, the streaker was big news around campus.

I called four of the main players into my office. They respectfully took off their hats and sat down. I was not kind to them, ripping them up one side and down the other. I told them that I was disappointed that they would treat someone this way, it was not acceptable, probably illegal, blah blah. They were looking down at their boots, without much to say.

I then asked what they thought any decent human being would have done if they even saw something like this happening.   Seriously, and sounding real sincere, Andy stated that "I gotta admit not giving the idiot the money after he did it was real tight. We should get him his money back." Mike added that "Fifty-two bucks is a lot of dough. I'da done it for seventy-five."

This was not the answer I was hoping for, but it did make a shred of horse sense. Nonetheless, I started over, talking about taking advantage of those less fortunate and making fun of folks as real disgusting entertainment. I threatened them with all sorts of things. They'll probably get suspended. I'm not sure they got my message. I'm not sure I shouldn't make them get the fifty-two bucks for Frankie.

Excuse Me! 'I went to the Health Department for a you-know-what test.'

State Champs

It has been exactly one year since our girls' basketball team won the state championship in the Oakland Coliseum Arena. The things I remember best are:

- How our tall Red Bluff girls looked so small in the Oakland Coliseum Arena.

- How cocky and confident the Southern California champs' players and coaches were during warmups.

- Seeing dozens of "fans" make the trip to Oakland who had never been to a home game.

- A star player's long lost father showing up and demanding a free ticket.

- Another father telling the tourney director he was the Red Bluff principal so he could get a front row seat.

- The tourney director, seeing my school jacket, asking me if I knew the "asshole Red Bluff principal" who demanded a front row seat.

- Having nearly everyone bitch and crab about where our rooting section was assigned to sit.

- Being proud, yet embarrassed, with everyone congratulating me, since I hadn't done much to get us there.

- One of the referees telling me that it was a pleasure working the game because our girls played so hard and were so polite.

- Our talented college prospects running into the stands like little girls to hug their families after the game.

- Seeing RED BLUFF DIV II STATE CHAMPS on the huge screen above center court.

The things I can't remember include:

- The final score.

- How many thousands of dollars the whole thing cost the school.

- Who, besides the referee and players, didn't complain about something.

Excuse Me! 'A tree squirrel knocked out the electricity.'

Aw Nesta Gawd This Really Happened

American Schools

We have had a German foreign exchange student living with us this past school year. It has been a great experience for all concerned. Julia is a delightful young woman, so it was no surprise that her parents are fine people. They visited us for graduation. Speaking very good English, they enjoyed visiting our school on several occasions and then attended the graduation ceremony.

Not unlike other exchange students, Julia did not find our school very difficult. She was the top student in calculus, chemistry, spoke three languages and so on. Sort of reinforced all that bashing our public schools get in the media when we are compared to Germany, Japan, Mars, Our Lady of Holy Anchovy and whoever.

Also, like other exchange students, she thoroughly enjoyed our social and extracurricular activities; most of which were not available in German schools. Julia, and her parents too, were truly excited about the athletic awards, prom photos, senior trip and all that stuff that probably gets in the way of our academically matching the foreign competition. I wasn't surprised, since they are gracious people and also said they really enjoyed Disneyland.

However, I was shocked when Julia's father told me how impressed he was with American public schools. He's a doctor, well educated and traveled man, who I am sure has seen the documented academic comparisons. With that comment, I also suspected that he might be a smart ass. Or maybe he had another daughter who needed a host family in America.

Maybe because I must have appeared to not believe him, he elaborated on our wonderful system from his point of view. It was his contention that our schools know how to teach the culture and values, while German schools only know academics. Germany has relied on family, church and tradition – or during the Nazi era an out of control government - to teach its young people values and socialization. Perhaps an education system with a social conscience would have provided balance to Hitler's Youth.

Germany is now experiencing an influx of refugees from Yugoslavia, Romania, the Balkans and other parts of Eastern Europe, not to mention the need to assimilate the East Germans. There are also the ugly seeds of a negative reaction. He sees no system for teaching these people how to be German and no way for Germans to learn to tolerate differences. He fears the inability of their society to peacefully assimilate new people and ideas may have grave and all too familiar consequences.

While certainly a painful process, American schools, he said, have done this with people from all parts of the world. We may have sacrificed some academic punch, but we have created and maintained a tolerant, inclusive and flexible system that has allowed us to remain a free people and world power. Hmm. This German guy may have something there. His comments certainly got me to wondering who's measuring and comparing what and maybe even what's really important after all the tests are scored.

It also got me thinking how this German view was a no-brainer and what an idiot I was for not having figured it out myself. My own parents didn't know a lick of English and never heard of George Washington when they entered an American public school. It was the school experience that quickly made them as American as Italians ever get. As for Our Lady of Holy Anchovy's impressive scores, I am pretty sure they never recruited my parents or many other nontraditional types.

My German friend also was quick to point out that people from around the world flock to American universities for advanced study. And why shouldn't they? Products of American universities routinely garner most of the international awards for advanced study and research. He attributed this to an open educational system that promoted divergent thought and did not stifle creativity. In his view, lagging standardized test scores were a small price to pay.

Maybe you survey takers ought to go suck an egg. Or maybe go survey and test the Chinese, Croatians, Albanians or Martians. And, while you are doing the survey, ask them some questions about things that really matter. My German friend was quick to point out that many of the young skinhead neo-nazis in Europe are quite well educated by academic standards.

American public schools may be one of the better parts of America. In this day and age, the blamers may not find this politically correct, but it just might be the ugly truth. Take it from my German friend.

"Rarely is the question asked; is our children learning?"

- George W. Bush

Excuse Me! 'I had three tests, so I stayed home and worried.'

The Stupidest Questions I Asked and the Answers
I Didn't Get

Students

Question: Did any of you see who threw the firecracker?
Answer:

Question: How many of you would like to go straight home after the game and not stop to eat?
Answer:

Question: Does anyone know who was on the cleanup committee?
Answer:

Question: Why didn't you guys think about going to the bathroom *before* we got on the bus?
Answer:

Question: Does anyone know who ate the doughnuts for the faculty meeting?
Answer:

Faculty

Question: Would any of you like to be cheerleader advisor?
Answer:

Question: Are there any faculty volunteers for rest room supervision?
Answer:

Question: Do any of you have classes with too few students?
Answer:

Question: Does anyone want to be on the student dress code committee?
Answer:

Excuse Me! 'My mother's getting married again and I helped her pack for the honeymoon.'

Aw Nesta Gawd This Really Happened

Pass the Phenol

The longer I'm in this business, the more I appreciate and enjoy the youngest teachers. The ones teaching English have yet to meet the Christian Fundamentalists, who'll bash them for teaching 'Of Mice and Men,' a vulgar tool of Satan. The ones in wood shop haven't had a kid saw off an index finger. The ones who coach haven't been forced out for not winning 'em all. They haven't been named a defendant in a frivolous lawsuit. They still think the public appreciates everything they do.

Which brings me to Jessica, our first year science teacher. Full of enthusiasm, she wants her students to love science. There will be no boring 'read the chapter, answer the questions' in her class. It will be hands on, experiments and fun stuff, just like the research and her professors say it should be. Her freshmen students do like science and she loves teaching.

However, yesterday she inadvertently took a step toward answering the questions at the end of the chapter. Her class was doing a fun experiment that she'd spent a lot of time setting up. Her class was making some jello-like stuff designed to show some scientific theory. One of the ingredients was phenolphthalein. So far, so good.

It might have been okay if she hadn't taken time to elaborate on the ingredients. Telling freshmen that phenolphthalein is a mild laxative got little minds spinning. Frankie just happened to have a bag of hard candy in his backpack. In an instant, he and Mario were rolling the candy in the solution and re-wrapping it in the paper it came in. With characteristic enthusiasm, Jessica was too busy explaining the experiment to notice what they were up to.

At break, Frankie and Mario, being the generous boys they are, were handing out candy to all their unsuspecting friends and anyone else who expressed an interest. From there, the events were quite predictable. Several excited girls rushed into the office saying that two boys were handing out candy laced with some drug. Some said it was LSD. One said it was cyanide.

All of a sudden, students were saying they were sick, others were calling home, parents were calling the school, vice principals were grilling witnesses, the school nurse was on the poison hot line, Frankie and Mario were sobbing and Jessica was horrified. The science lesson might have missed the mark, but no one was accusing Jessica of inciting boredom.

Before school was out, the frenzy had subsided. I don't know of anyone who was actually sick, even though some students went home under their grumpy mothers' cozy wings. Frankie and Mario were amply scared and tortured by all involved. Jessica seemed shaken, but okay, even when the smart ass vice principal tossed a handful of candy on her desk after school.

Excuse Me! 'I had to help Mom slop the hogs.'

Stupidest Questions By Taxpayers and
Other Experts

Question: How have you wasted the millions of lottery dollars?
Answer: I took my secretary out to lunch at Burger King and told the kid behind the counter to keep the change.

Question: Do you know what your kids are doing on Halloween night?
Answer: Well, actually, my kids are here at home and I frankly don't give a dink what your or someone else's kids are doing at eleven at night.

Question: Would you tell the kid in the black shirt that he should not throw trash on my lawn on his way home from school?
Answer: Well sure, we have only eighty-seven kids here today with black shirts and we'll administer the lie detector test right after first period.

Question: We need guys like you in our Raccoon Club. . . lot of good contacts there, Joe. How about coming aboard at our next meeting?
Answer: Now, I sincerely appreciate you guys running the beer booth at the fair and donating the proceeds to our drug and alcohol abuse program, but I'd rather eat my lunch with teenagers.

Question: I'm the youth minister at the new church and feel church leaders need to show visible support for our youth. Could you check with your boss and get me a pass to your athletic events?
Answer: As soon as your Big Boss comes through with a lot more money for schools, I plan to give every single minister an engraved free pass.

Question: What's it like being a principal?
Answer: It's kinda like being the caretaker in a cemetery – you have a lot of people under you, but no one's listening.

Question: Mr. Piper grew up here in Red Bluff, you know. Why don't you hire a local boy, one of our own, as basketball coach?
Answer: That idiot who kept a sex slave in a box grew up here also. We're not hiring him either.

"Managing is getting paid for home runs that someone else hits."
- Casey Stengel

Excuse Me! 'My father was drinking again last night. I don't go home when he's drinking'

Aw Nesta Gawd This Really Happened

George

I swear, if George dies, we'll need to hire two custodians to replace him. George is the eighty something neighbor who spends every day scavengering our campus for anything recyclable. He hauls off sacks of garbage that he once told me helps pay for his ailing wife's medicine. Quiet and shy, he also timidly comes into the office on occasion with coats or books he's found or to report some strange happenings on campus. He calls us when he finds a door unsecured. What a guy! I'm not going to be the one who tells him he causes too many problems.

The first George crisis had to do with someone, who mustn't have enough to do, wondering about liability, workmen's comp and that stuff. What if George is trampled by the lunchtime rush to the cafeteria? What if George cuts himself on a pop top? What if some nasty kid stuffs him in a garbage can? So we turned in all the paperwork to the DO and made George an official volunteer. We gave him a school ball cap, which he wears every day. This volunteer stuff didn't set well with the union, although they didn't say much, maybe because George works harder than most members.

Next, George pissed off the special education department. It seems that the severely handicapped class had collected aluminum cans to fund its end of the year picnic. George is quite adept at knowing the hot spots and probably a bit quicker than the special ed students, hence they often finished second in their quest for cans. They were willing to share, however, until a sack of cans turned up missing from their classroom. For them, George was the obvious culprit, although I suspected he just thought it payment for securing their door one too many times. A confrontation was averted when another funding source for the picnic was miraculously discovered.

A science teacher then equated the impending flu epidemic with George's routine of going through garbage cans and then touching other things like door knobs and drinking fountain handles. For me, this seemed a bit paranoid, given what several thousand teenagers routinely touch in a day's activity. Nonetheless, in response to the germ phobia, we outfitted George with rubber gloves, instructing him to use one hand in the garbage and the other to open doors, etc. We told George it was a state law or something and since no one died from the flu, everyone was semi-satisfied.

The latest George fiasco has to do with two elderly ladies in the neighborhood who want to know why George has the franchise on our recyclable garbage. Apparently, they confronted George on campus and it wasn't a pretty sight. It's a public school and they pay taxes and they've probably got stories even better than George's ailing wife. George is not sympathetic. The women suggest dividing the campus into zones or alternating days. I'm not telling George he's out of business. Good grief, we need the guy, his wife needs the medicine. I suggest going out to the dump and hauling in more garbage. If these women hurt George, he at least has workmen's comp.

Excuse Me! 'I joined the carnival for a week, but those carnies are weird, so I'm back.'

This is a guest article submitted by Mickey Bitsko, an old friend of our principal.

The All-Attitude Team

The Daily News Holiday Classic is a classic because of attitude. Like the mural on the wall says, 'Attitude Is Everything!' Trust me, talent and brains are overrated. It's the people with the get-it-done attitudes who put the 'class' in Classic. The custodian who watches for a single burned out bulb in the scoreboard or the mother who makes the dynamite Hospitality Room chili every year. Red Bluff has dozens of folks with the right attitude.

The same goes for the players on the court. A few have talent and a great attitude. They have everything and are special. They were lucky to be born with the talent and even luckier to have learned the attitude. These few will be respected by teammates, coaches and fans all the way to the top.

We all also have a favorite story or two about the talented player with the big stats and bozo attitude who ended up leading the city league in 'T''s. While their talent got them on every all-tourney team, we knew all along they were better suited for the all-idiot five. They couldn't figure out the attitude and won't figure out much else in life.

So not everyone can have talent, but anyone with a heart and willingness to work, can have the attitude. How about the player who competes ferociously and fairly from tip-off to buzzer? Or the benchwarmer who spends thirty minutes jumping to his or her feet encouraging teammates and two minutes diving for loose balls after the outcome of the game is decided? Or the guy who religiously keeps stats for 24 straight games? These deserve to be on an All-Attitude Team.

The people on an All-Attitude Team could someday orchestrate a tourney like this one. In fact, since they know attitude is everything, they will be able to do almost anything they choose. Schools spout off about values, sportsmanship and attitudes in high school athletics, but most tourneys are stuck with an All-Tourney Team based on stats and talent. That's hypocritical, at best.

Last year, the Holiday Classic broke the mold. It wasn't easy. Traditional All-Tourney teams are simple. God picked them 17 or 18 years ago when she handed out the talent. Media folks verify them by adding up the numbers. Coaches and tourney officials have to think a bit about what they value to figure out the Holiday Classic All-Attitude Team.

- Mickey Bitsko

Excuse Me! '**She has a bad attitude about going to school. I'm sending her to live with her father.**'

72

Aw Nesta Gawd This Really Happened

Peters

The rallies have been well attended, exciting and positive. Having good kids helps. They are the best around. The focus has been on class competition with great participation. The winning class gets the spirit sword. Great rallies. Whoopee!

Someone said class competition could get out of hand. It hasn't , but what if they start sabotaging each other's Homecoming floats and stuff. Maybe we are lucky; those things happen, you know. So we are real smart; let's have a rally where class competition is not the focus. How about a battle of the sexes? The girls on one side of the gym and the guys on the other. What an idea!

The week before the rally there's plenty of enthusiasm for the competition. They're doing skits, costumes, whatever. Are we nervous? Yes, very. Those of us in the main office have heard the rumors about phallic symbols in the skits and references to feminine hygiene products. But they are good kids and they've heard the lectures.

Would you believe an area newspaper has heard about our school spirit and is going to do a feature on us? Are we nervous? YES! Hey, but they are good kids and they heard the lectures. Never mind that many of my favorite faculty members were taking delight in fabricating rumors and relaying them to me.

A thousand teens headed for the gym, the band was playing the school fight song, most were dressed in green and gold, lots of excitement about the big playoff game. There was a banner saying TESTOSTERONE RULES and some skinny freshmen girls had one saying WE ARE WOMEN - HEAR US! Hey, but no big deal.

The whole rally went pretty well. Toward the end, the girls started the popular taunt "Spirit, spirit, we got spirit. How 'bout you?" The other half of the gym answered even louder. The goofy looking boy cheerleaders had them going. Then I listened a bit more closely. Our male cherubs were actually chanting "Peters, peters. we got peters. How 'bout you?" A bit clever, yes, but not what a principal likes to hear. It ended with no ugly incidents and they emptied the gym. All in all, a good rally, with the girls a clear winner in the spirit competition. The newspaper guys left. I guess they got a story.

I headed for my office and wasn't there ten minutes when I got a phone call that went something like this: "This is Reverend Cox (Cocks?) and I'm calling about the reference to "peters" at the rally. I don't approve; my daughter was offended, blah, blah, blah." Now I'm sitting there with the phone in my ear thinking that some of my good friends on the staff are in another office, calling me and laughing like hell.

My instincts tell me to say something obscene and hang up. Why give them any satisfaction? But I'm chicken, so I listen and explain that it was in poor taste and certainly not expected or authorized. The Reverend thanked me and hung up.

Excuse Me! 'My mother had a nervous breakdown.'

Aw Nesta Gawd This Really Happened

Full Moon Friday

It was one of those full moon Fridays. The wackos were coming out of the woodwork. I was helping the stressed vice principal, who was preoccupied with a major drug bust. The police officer was in his office cataloging the pipes, dope and writing citations. Witnesses were blubbering in the next office.

Mrs. Wills called the office and excitedly reported to me that there was a major altercation in her science class. Petey was on his way to the office for fighting.   He was a huge boy of about 275 pounds - not as big as his mother - but huge, nonetheless. He was always fighting, it seemed. According to his mother, the punks in school picked on him all the time because he was bigger than they. I suspected there was more to it than that. Mom told me I needed to see a psychiatrist when I told her what I suspected.

Mrs. Wills knew to send Alan, the other combatant, down to the office after a fifteen minute wait, since the two obviously hadn't settled their differences when Petey was told to leave. Sweating profusely, Petey was slumped in a chair in the small ante room next to the vice principal's office. He was demanding medical attention for the scratch on his arm. I waited near the main office door for Alan's arrival.

Skinny and probably less than half Petey's weight, Alan was a regular with the vice principal, so he knew the way.   He didn't enter through the main door, but sidled in through a side door into the vice principal's ante room. Consequently, I didn't see him. My first clues that he had arrived were a very loud thump on the ante room wall, a framed picture hitting the floor and a chair flying out into the main office. By the time I got in there, Alan was on top of Petey pummeling him about the head and shoulders, while Petey was unsuccessfully trying to flee. Both were screaming obscenities, tearing each other's clothes and knocking chairs and wall hangings in all directions.

Luckily the policeman, who was next door, reacted to the commotion much more quickly than me. Some would say I was intentionally lethargic in responding, but I firmly believe it was his extensive training that got him there first. Whatever the reason, he had burst through the door and was ordering Alan to stop.

Alan was possessed and heard not a word, so the policeman grabbed him and tried to restrain him. Petey got away and ran into the main office. The policeman, in his firmest cop voice, ordered Alan to settle down. Alan responded by continuing his screaming and flailing and popping the policeman in the chops. This was not a good idea. Quick as a flash, the policeman had Alan face down, on the floor, his hands behind him and was getting his handcuffs ready to secure Alan's hands behind his back.

Alan continued to thrash and yell, even when cuffed. The policeman calmly told him about his being arrested for fighting, resisting arrest and assaulting an officer. Alan finally sat down in one of the chairs I righted. He was still grumbling about his rights and that the cop was picking on him just like Petey had been. Self defense, he protested. He knew his rights. We needed to call his mother. The policeman left me there with Alan and went back to the drug bust.

After about 15 minutes, Alan seemed to quiet down, so I headed across the office to my desk. I told one of the secretaries to keep an eye on him. Dutifully, Joan ran in to tell me that Alan was doing something weird on the floor. I hurried over to find him lying on the floor on his back, rocking back and forth, in a fetal position. He was trying to get the cuffs around to his front, but had only gotten them down under his knees. He was begging me to rescue him, but I told him he'd have to stay put. The cop had the keys and he was busy.

In the meantime, Petey's mother had been called and told to pick up her son one more time for fighting. She huffed and puffed up the front stairs, outfitted in yards and and yards of pink polyester. She burst into the office demanding to know what we did to the other kid. She'd forgotten her teeth and was not easy to understand, which was just as well, since she wasn't saying nice things. Petey pointed to the other kid handcuffed, rocking back and forth, in the fetal position, on the ante room floor. That seemed to satisfy her and for the first time she left without calling any of us the usual names.

I had left Alan there on the floor while I went to take a phone call. Joan came back in to tell me Alan had gotten one leg out and was inching toward his backpack on the other side of the small room. I trotted back, and, sure enough, through some contortionist move, he had gotten his cuffed hands in front of him and was crawling toward his backpack, which we'd placed in a corner chair.

I had visions of a weapon in the backpack, so I grabbed for it just before he got to it. Alan started screaming something about Jesus Christ and the Bible. I talked him back into the chair and then opened the backpack. There were no weapons, not even school books in it, just a large Bible. He said he just wanted to read it. I told him to shut up and wait and that he should have read the good book before he hammered Petey and the cop.

Not long thereafter, the policeman came back and led Alan and the cuffed dope dealer to the patrol car and put them in the back seat for the short ride to juvenile hall. An hour or so later Alan's mother showed up at school. She was a semi-nice looking lady, crying and obviously upset that the police had called to tell of her son's whereabouts and the charges.

She immediately told me that she couldn't even see Alan; they had him in solitary confinement. She said he was new to our school, took five medications, had three doctors, an IEP and that this behavior was part of his handicapping condition. As such, she forthrightly informed me that we could not suspend him as a result of actions derived from this handicapping condition. She suspected that her son hadn't taken his medication because he was so upset that his father had gone back to jail. She'd been through this at his other school and she knew her rights. She had the phone numbers of all of his doctors, plus his special ed advocate.

I told her that Alan, in fact, was not suspended. We hadn't had time to even think about it. However, I mentioned she should know that the police had no clue about IEP's and didn't give a rip about handicapping conditions. It was just not a good idea to punch a cop, no matter what your school IEP said, but she could use my phone to call anyone she wanted. She declined and finally seemed to understand that there was nothing I could do or anyone I could call that would get Alan out of the slammer.

She actually began to think I was on her side in this debacle, while, in fact, I was damn glad the cop had hauled her son off and locked him up. The cop probably saved me from being hurt by a kid's handicapping condition. I would have probably gotten a black eye or worse, defending a 275 pound bully and it would have been my fault. She stopped crying and we became friends of a sort. She even asked my advice. I told her that my best advice would be to have a kid with an IEP punch a principal rather than a cop. She looked at me strangely and left.

Full moon Fridays can be a bitch.

Young and Old

All people have something in common as far as age goes. All were once younger and all are getting older. The younger ones see themselves as individuals trying to lead their own lives, while older ones see the younger ones as making the same mistakes they made. Who is right? I can't answer that question yet because I haven't experienced both sides of the story.

Or have I?

- Tina

Excuse Me! 'My aunt dropped a bowling ball on my foot.'

Aw Nesta Gawd This Really Happened

Pee

The high school rest room is a special place. "Rest room supervision" has to be the most common topic on administrative meeting agendas. There's some real action in those places. I have always felt that the quickest way to assess a high school is to look around the student rest room. At the very least, you can always check the walls and find out the principal's name. You can usually also find out the current smoke and drink of choice.

We are with students in the classroom, the cafeteria, at dances, games and everywhere else. Yet we leave the rest rooms as sacred teenage sanctuaries. One of the simple things we could do to improve schools (in my opinion) would be to get rid of the staff bathrooms. Teachers would still have to recycle their coffee somewhere, so they would use the student rest rooms. This would certainly discourage much of the abnormal activity that takes place in these deviant dens.

In addition to that, there is something about urinating in front of others (as males are prone to do) that creates a common level of respect that is hard to duplicate in any other setting. I remember a friend of mine traveling to Washington D.C. and visiting Congress. A history buff, he visited the Senate floor, the Congressional committees and the offices of his own Senators and Representative. Yet he swears that standing at a urinal peeing next to Hubert Humphrey changed his view of American politics, the world and his whole life. They didn't talk, just peed. That was it, changed his life.

Perhaps teachers could have a similar effect on kids. Males do weird things at the urinal. Just the other day, I went into the student rest room and walked up to a urinal between two little freshmen, who I could see looking at me out of the corner of their eyes. They were talking before I arrived, but were now awkwardly silent as they stood there aiming at those little white cake things. Finally one of them said to the other, "Hey Tommy, what do you think about Yeltsin?" Tommy replied, "Don't know, but do you think that cold front is going to get here?"

They then quickly zipped up their pants and left. I never said a thing and have no idea why they said what they did. I doubt that they were talking politics and weather before I got there. They were just jerking my chain, I guess. It didn't change my life and probably not theirs, but it certainly altered their behavior. We should be in there more often. I know it would make a difference, at least on the boys' side.

I am certainly less familiar and much less certain about the female situation. They don't have the lineup type thing as the great equalizer. I guess it's much more private and, who knows, Hillary Clinton may not even go to the bathroom. However, it couldn't hurt since the stories that come out of the ladies' room are even more bizarre than their male counterparts.

Excuse Me! 'I had to take my dog to the vet. He couldn't go by himself; he doesn't know the way.

Aw Nesta Gawd This Really Happened

Rah-Rah Nazis

There is a word that will make every high school principal in America quiver. That word is 'cheerleader.' It was when I attended the World Conference of Principals in Sydney, Australia that I realized that American principals have the toughest administrative assignment on the planet. No one else, from Taiwan to Tasmania, has to deal with cheerleaders.

I'd be sitting around a table with principals from South Africa, Sweden, Germany, The Philippines, wherever, and we were all amazed at the worldwide similarities in issues for principals. Mention grading systems, teacher unions, state testing or most anything else and there would be acknowledging nods and instant chatter. Mutter the word cheerleader and, if there was another American, they'd roll their eyes and gasp. The others would look puzzled and ask for a definition. Try to explain that one in an hour or less and not have the whole world think you're an idiot.

Actually, it is not the cheerleaders themselves. Most are beautiful, bright-eyed and charming - most of the time. Even the goofy male ones, like Alex, who insisted on riding his white, and very wild, steed around the stadium after touchdowns, aren't that bad. Most are talented and very athletic and it's not even the problems that arise. It's their damn mothers.

Something happens to ordinary looking women when their daughters try out for cheerleading. They become Rah-Rah Nazis. Whatever the selection process, it is doomed to venomous criticism. Whoever the advisor, she can do no right and is doomed to personal slurs and vicious attacks. I have never met a potential cheerleader mother who thought her daughter might not be good enough to make the cheerleading squad.

Principals instinctively and selfishly support and coddle their cheerleader advisors, regardless of competence. They see them as the first line of defense against the mothers. They know who'll get bashed if they blow it on the front line. They know that Rah-Rah Nazis travel in groups and attack in packs. It's not a pretty sight. So it's "Go! Fight! Win! for the Advisor."

Unfortunately, cheerleading advisors don't win often and have a very short life span. Their resignation letters always have a disclaimer about how they "love the kids, but . . . " I know what they mean. At one point, I had eleven former cheerleader advisors on staff. I had only been there ten years. One included a vice principal with an emergency assignment, who promised to do "anything, absolutely anything," if I'd hire a regular cheerleader advisor.

I know this sounds sexist, but it's always the mothers. I have only encountered one cheerleader father. He was a lawyer and I was paranoid as hell when he made an appointment. Turns out, he wanted me to tell his daughter that if her grades didn't come up she'd find "those pom-poms shoved where the sun doesn't shine." I complied, restated it, but enthusiastically complied.

This sounds impossible, I know, but I rarely understand what the Rah-Rah Nazis are fired up about. It can be tryouts, fairness, uniforms or what someone said someone said. My comprehension probably has nothing to do with their not clearly presenting the gripe. They say it to my face. They say it loudly. They say it in writing. They say it at the hairdresser's. It's my paranoia. These women scare me. I get nervous and don't listen well. I just want them to simmer down. I want to get through it because I know it won't be the end. Another pack is revving up.

Athletic coaches are no help. For whatever reason, they are nearly unanimous, even the female ones, in not wanting cheerleaders riding team buses. Maybe they think they are too pretty, a distraction or something. Maybe they know their mothers. At best, they are uncooperative. Trust me, you'll never hear a coach say, "Hey great, the cheerleaders are riding with us."

A cheerleading squad was once left at the curb by two football coaches. Seems three freshmen cheerleaders had forgotten their jackets and run back to their lockers. The coaches told the bus driver to leave them all. Did I meet some mothers or what?! They were not happy, even though I drove their daughters to the game in a van. This was too little, too late. Their daughters were crushed. Their mascara was a mess. On and on.

Looking back, it could have been worse. My own daughters were never interested in cheerleading, so their mother pursued other passions. A good friend tells about having a cheerleading daughter while principal. It was not the daughter who disrupted household harmony. It was his wife whom he finally insisted make an appointment at school if she wanted to discuss cheerleading with the principal.

Short of moving to Tasmania, I see no relief. Cheerleaders are here to stay. Rah-Rah Nazis are occupational hazards. Live with it.

"Don't look back. Something might be gaining on you."

- Satchel Paige

Excuse Me! 'I think the cafeteria food poisoned me.'

Student Body Politics

Mr. Pelanconi
Principal
Red Bluff High School

Dear Mr. Pelanconi:

I would like to apologize to you if any of my campaign speech for student body president was offensive in your opinion. It was brought to my attention that if I win, there could be some concern how I would represent the school.

I saw Jay Leno make fun of the woman who did that awful thing to her husband with a butcher knife, so I thought that the chopping of the cucumber would be entertaining to the students. I really had no intentions of offending anyone and give you my word I will do the very best job if elected.

Sincerely,

Aw Nesta Gawd This Really Happened

Where's Annie?

You've got to love Annie. She's one of those kids with bright eyes, a quick smile and great attitude. She's sharp as a tack and eager to please. Her parents are supportive and cooperative. She's very Red Bluff; a perfect example of why working here is a pleasure. She's also naive as hell.

Annie loved Rome. All of the exchange group did. Their eyes were wide open, so much to see. St. Peter's, the Sistine Chapel, Roman Forum, Colosseum - and those were just the tourist attractions. Subways, trains, city busses, thousands of mopeds, Vespas and Fiats, all with crazy Italian drivers were even bigger wonders. We don't see stuff like that back home.

They followed Sue and me everywhere in a weird formation. They reminded us of auction cattle, in the pen during the sale, bumping into each other and trying to look in all directions at once. Everything was new, exciting and a bit scary. The five million Romans move at a hectic pace. Our group moved much more slowly and we always seemed to be in the way.

For me, these usually confident and cocky kids were rather fascinating and somewhat amusing The teacher in me saw it as one of those prime learning moments. These country kids were out of their comfort zone and absorbing everything like little sponges. No one was bored and dozing off. Educators live for these moments. Then we lost Annie.

We were on a city bus. We were to get off and walk to Piazza Navona. The bus was crowded. I yelled for everybody to get off at the next stop. The bus whipped up to the curb. Twenty five of us got off, dragging backpacks and cameras. The doors slammed shut and the bus raced off into eight lanes of traffic - with Annie's face plastered to the door's window glass. We all saw the strickened look on her face. She could have been screaming, but we couldn't hear her.

It seems Annie was politely letting other folks go before her. That works in Red Bluff. Dammit, we had talked about this sort of thing. Hey, but not to worry. I'm a trained professional. Let's remain calm and go to plan B. Sue can take the group to Piazza Navona and I'll run down to the next bus stop and pick up Annie. This will be a great object lesson on city life. We can have a nice little lesson right in front of Bernini's fountain in Piazza Navona. Maybe now they'll believe me when I say we're not in Kansas anymore.

Well, it seems Annie did actually get off at the next stop, but she forgot to hug a tree. She took off running to catch us, but went the wrong way. When you're from Red Bluff, Rome can do that to you (so can Chico, for that matter). When I got there, no Annie.   I then headed for the Colosseum, the bus destination, since she knew we were headed there eventually. No Annie.

I was now more than a little bit nervous. I hiked to the train station, since she must have remembered that we'd end up there. It was a long walk. Long enough for me to ponder how frightened Annie must be. I also had to keep suppressing imagined phone conversations with her parents. "Annie was having a great time, but we lost her. . ." There was the superintendent and the school board. They were going to take a dim view of this turn of events. I gave some thought to my next career. Tour guide was definitely not at the top of my list.

No Annie at the train station. It was like this monster city had stolen her and fed her to the lions. Just to add some Italian charm, the busses and subway folks went on strike while I was at the station. I took a cab back to Piazza Navona, where Sue and the group were stranded. I tried real hard to appear calm and in total control. Apparently, I wasn't too good at it, since no one was talking much as the group trudged to the Colosseum. I headed back to the train station. I had to pretend I was doing something.

At the station, I called our host school in Florence. Yes, they had heard about Annie. Whew! The American Embassy had found their number in Annie's backpack and called them. With typical Italian flair for crises, most of the students at the host school were in varying stages of emotional distress. Annie was rapidly becoming a celebrity in Florence. Italians love bambini and go to great lengths to worry and take care of them. Losing one was not good. Consequently, I was becoming a celebrity of a quite different sort.

It seems that Annie had gotten completely confused. In her words, "I lost it, sup, sup, I lost it big time." She was sobbing nonstop and couldn't make any of the Italians who tried to help her understand where she was going. An Australian couple tried to help, but they didn't know anything about Rome either. The Aussies did find some caribineri, who took her to the police station. She cried a lot there, while the police tried to find an English interpreter. Finally, they just hauled her to the American Embassy.

When I got to the Embassy, Annie was very red eyed, her hair in disarray and that quick smile had a curled lower lip. In between sup sups, she had been eating gnocchi and telling the Embassy staff about Red Bluff. Annie was ecstatic when she saw me, perhaps even happier than I was to see her. It had been a very long afternoon for both of us. When we rejoined the group at the train station, Annie got a hero's welcome, flowers and all. No formal lesson was needed. They held hands a lot after that.

Next year, we are going to rehearse some city stuff before we go - how to push, shove and be rude. We'll have bus evacuation drills. We'll all carry city maps and know how to use them. We'll learn some basic Italian phrases. We'll have important phone numbers tattooed on our arms and we'll know how to use Italian phones. It will be like scrimmages before the big game.

Those are good ideas. We might even do some of them, but for some reason I think we'll still look like auction yard cattle.

Excuse Me! 'Someone was in my parking space, so I went home.'

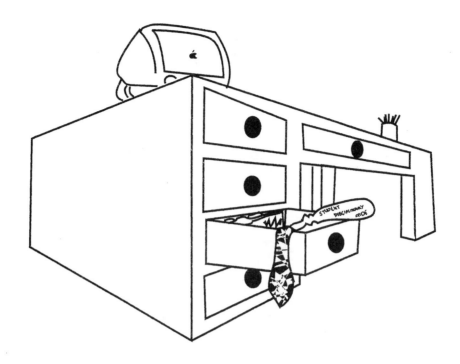

Another Drawer

This drawer contains items that suggest that Joe had finally accepted his plight as a semi-respectable principal and was even enjoying the ride. The late 80's and early 90's were good times in his school, which is to say he probably wasn't as 'interim' as he would have hoped.

M.B.

It's the Crab Season

Dear Bluffer Staff:

Would you guys quit ragging on me about writing this column for *The Bluffer*? Julie keeps sending me nasty little notes about deadlines and stuff. It's your darn paper. Can't you clowns think of anything to write? We pay your adviser, Mrs. Franklin, a BIG salary - get her to fill up some space!

Don't you know that I'm real busy this time of year? This is the crab season. Everyone's real crabby. I don't need any more pressure from you idiots. Teachers are tired and grumpy. The office staff has seen one too many forged attendance notes. Custodians are sick and tired of getting the pizza off the floor in Room 315. Underclassmen are worried about grades, summer jobs, elections and their oh-so-important social lives.

And the seniors! Boy, are they a pain! They want a first class graduation, senior breakfast, sober grad party, scholarships, letters of recommendation and advice on what to do next year. They are stressed about graduating, leaving home, going to college, getting a job and that kind of stuff. They are getting real crabby.

Hey, you know what? This all might be normal. The seniors might have good reasons to be a little wired and weird. Perhaps they even need our support. They've been a great class. I could probably lighten up a bit and help send our seniors out of here with tons of enthusiasm and a positive attitude.

You know, I really could do that. Maybe a supportive attitude would be contagious. How about if we all chill out and end the school year on real upbeat? This could be a great discovery - a cure for the crab season.

What the heck, I could even write a dumb column for *The Bluffer*. It's a great student newspaper and your staff works really hard. Julie is a very nice person. You probably also could use some support this time of year. I'll get right on it.

Sincerely,

Mr. Pelanconi

Too Good to Be True

Rachel

There are some kids that are just too good to be true. I don't know where they come from. I suspect they are sent by the guardian angel for principals. Nearly every year, there's at least one who reassures you that the whole thing is worthwhile.

This year it's Rachel. The youngest of a number of sisters, raised by a single mom in humble and often confusing circumstances, Rachel is special. Quiet, rather ordinary looking and not a top student, the kid is amazing. Her ability to instantly assess where people are coming from and make them feel comfortable is uncanny.

It's not just me who's noticed. She was elected Student Body President, Homecoming Queen and most everything else. She's a kid who never, ever draws attention to herself, yet commands instant respect. She is so sincere, sensitive and forceful that people just listen. She appears embarrassed when thrust into a leadership role, but proceeds with a calm confidence that's eluded me after 25 years of practice.

Rachel talks to the freshmen, convinces them they are adults and an important part of the school. She says it in a quiet, straight forward manner with a shy smile, telling them how frightened she was as a freshman coming from a one room elementary school. They appear mesmerized and believe everything she says. She did it to the faculty when I had her address them. She apologized for not having notes and being disorganized, but explained that notes were useless when speaking from the heart.

She talks with the mayor, convincing him that the City Council can help youth by supporting such events as Homecoming or the Basketball Tourney. He walks out of their meeting shaking his head and says to me "Boy, was I overmatched!"

Rachel was a tireless volunteer on the bond election. She worked the phone banks, helped with the mailings, but it was personal appearances that were incredible. She'd smile and quietly tell the Chamber of Commerce how proud they should be of their high school. They probably voted 'No,' but it wasn't her fault. They loved her. Someone suggested we put her photo on the campaign mailings. We should have.

On election day, Rachel walked by my office, flashed her shy smile and gave me the thumbs up sign. The next day, she stopped by my office to thank me for allowing her to be part of the election and offer whatever support I needed. She said she was sure that the landslide defeat was not a reflection on the school. She was absolutely certain we had the best school and principal in the world.

There was Homecoming Week, when she was working on floats, running for Queen, organizing events, keeping up school work and hardly sleeping. She came by my office on Thursday to tell me she understood how stressed I must be this week, but that she really appreciated all the support the administration had given the students.

I am not sure where she came from or why she's here, but I really do suspect there is a cosmic force working here on my behalf. I am also sure that another Rachel will come out of the woodwork right before it appears they're about to commit me.

Excuse Me! 'Columbus Day was a holiday at our last school.'

Too True to Be Good

Willard

Willard Dilbert from Red Bluff - it sounds like a name someone made up for a low budget western movie. That was really his name and he grew up in Red Bluff and so did most of his family. He was a senior and by his own admission he was on the verge of a miracle. He was close to getting a high school diploma. No one in his entire family - and it was a large one - had even come close. As he told me over and over, "They're depending on me and they're all coming to graduation."

Willard's high school career had not been a thing of beauty. He was an honest, well-meaning young man, but his performance was less than stellar. Furthermore, he possessed none of the social graces that might endear him to teachers so they might give him the benefit of the doubt. One might say he was a bit rough around the edges.

In spite of all this, Willard was down to his last semester and needed only to pass his classes and one additional night class to be the number one Dilbert scholar. He was staggering through his regular day classes, but was having no such luck with the evening venture. I had taken a special liking to Willard - maybe it was the name.

Visibly upset, Willard came into my office unannounced one day, with tears in his eyes, he took off his cowboy hat and plopped down in a chair. "I screwed it up good this time, Mr. Pelanconi" he said while looking at the floor. "How'd you manage that?" I inquired. "I called the night school teacher a 'stupid bitch'." "That'll do it," I assured him. "She doesn't want to ever see my ass again," he drawled. The teacher had made a lot of effort to accommodate Willard's style, and he was the first to acknowledge that. The final straw had to do with one more little misunderstanding. So here we were, the first Dilbert ever to have ordered a cap and gown and he wasn't going to be wearing it.

Luckily for Willard, Rick came in my door. As the vice principal in charge of attendance, Rick had ample reason to know the Dilberts. Willard told him the awful news. Rick asked him if the night school teacher was the same woman who worked at school during the day. Willard said it was, but that it was no use. She had given him plenty of chances and she was real mad this time. Rick told Willard there was one last hope and that he'd be right back. Rick returned in about 15 minutes with a single red rose. He told Willard that his last shot was to give the rose to her and look real sincere. Willard's response was, "You gotta be shittin' me." Rick assured him that he wasn't and with a little prodding, Willard headed out of my office with the red rose.

He was back in about five minutes and in a rather dazed state, he again plopped down in the chair and muttered "I fricking can't believe what I just did." I told him what he did wasn't too important - but what did she do? Shaking his head in disbelief, he said, "She gave me a big hug and told me she'd see me Tuesday night. Can you fricking believe that?"

Willard's whole family did indeed show up for graduation.

Excuse Me! 'My alarm clock biffed it. It blinked '12' all day long.'

87

Aw Nesta Gawd This Really Happened

Where's the Rat?

Mr. Warren is very serious about science. I am sure he got excellent grades in college. You wouldn't call his classes exciting, but there is no doubt that he is concerned about his students learning biology. His classroom is interesting, being home to a number of caged animals, including a large boa constrictor. He is also a very moral man with a clear definition of what is right and wrong.

Melissa is bright, pretty and quiet. She has many friends and no one would suspect that her family is into animal rights, particularly since they own a fast food hamburger restaurant. She seems to like school, receives decent grades and causes no problems in class. Or at least that is the way it appeared.

Every week Mr. Warren puts several live rats into the boa's cage. Teenagers, who tend to thrive on the macabre, usually enjoy watching the inevitable. Over the years, it has become an accepted part of what happens in Warren's science room and far more memorable than his genetics lecture. At $2.00 per rat, Mr. Warren sees the ritual as his personal contribution to experiential learning.

Last Thursday, one of the rats disappeared from the cage before the boa had lunch. Mr. Warren noticed almost immediately, but could not determine which student had opened the cage. Through an informant, he found out Friday that it was Melissa who had taken the rat. When confronted, Melissa acknowledged that she had the rat at home, but denied stealing it. In her words, she had "taken it into protective custody." She also stated that she had no intention of returning the rat so that it could be killed by the snake.

Mr. Warren caught me in my office Friday after school. For him, it was an open and closed case - petty theft and defiance - she admitted guilt on both counts. He wanted to know if the administration was going to call the police or deal with it through suspension or other in-house torture. I suggested that we deal with the issue Monday and that he could perhaps solve it by calling Melissa's parents. He was not happy when he left and I had the feeling I hadn't heard the last of the rat.

Later that evening, Melissa's mother called a vice principal, upset that we had a teacher who would promote such ghoulish behavior in the classroom. Obviously upset, she suggested such solutions as feeding Mr. Warren to the snake. She wholeheartedly supported her daughter's right to keep and save the rat's life. She was willing to involve animal rights groups, the media and anyone else to make her point. The vice principal suggested she do nothing until Monday when we had time to sort it out.

A loyal and obedient employee, Mr. Warren called Melissa's father that evening as suggested, informing him that the police, suspension, a failing grade were all suitable consequences for a thief. Melissa's father stated that the vice principal had already solved the problem and then proceeded to call Mr. Warren a 'sadist,' a 'sicko' , a 'dickhead' and a few other colorful and descriptive terms. By both accounts, the conversation did not end amicably.

Mr. Warren then called the vice principal back demanding to know why the administration had gone behind his back and cut a deal with a thief. This conversation ended abruptly, since the vice principal could not figure out what Warren was talking about.

Monday morning Melissa gave Mr. Warren a $5 bill. He took it and neither of them said a word. I am quite certain that no one is happy with the resolution, but I'm sure as hell not going to bring it up. However, some big-time questions do remain:

I) Does Melissa have $3.00 in change coming? Or does she have a rat and a half in credit?
2) What are the boa's rights? Is he hungry?
3) Is there any meat in the family's fast food burgers?
4) Do administrators care about rats, teachers or anything else?

Why Am I?

Why am I the person I am?
　　Could I dislike being you?

Why am I the color I am?
　　Could I not like yours the same?

Why do I act the way I do?
　　Could I not act the way you do?

Why do we live so close together,
　　But talk with different tongues?

Why are we so much unlike?

Is it impossible to be alike?

　　　　　　　　　　- Miguel

Excuse Me! 'Dibble Creek was 6 feet high and rising.'

Stupidest Questions Asked By Teachers and the Answer
I Didn't Give

Question: Is the 7:15 A.M. faculty meeting mandatory?
Answer: Oh no, it is just a device I use to find out who the ass kissers are.

Question: Is it true that you have to be a personal friend of the principal to get a computer in your classroom?
Answer: Well, actually, you must be an intimate friend of the principal. And since I am bisexual, this is a very fair policy.

Question: What's your policy on tardies?
Answer: Are you talking about students or teachers? For students, its a rather reasonable approach - usually a conference, simple consequence or a call to parents if it persists. I don't know what the hell to do with teachers who can't get their butts to class on time, since none of the above seems to work.

Question: Can I take my classroom VCR home for the summer?
Answer: Hey, of course you can. Just today I got a call from the Taxpayers Association wanting to know if you needed a school bus for your family's summer vacation.

Question: Does our bereavement leave pertain to family pets?
Answer: Only if you have listed them as a dependant on your medical insurance and they are the sole beneficiary on your life insurance policy.

Question: Is tenure optional?
Answer: What?

"You don't need a weatherman to know which way the wind blows.'
- Bob Dylan

Excuse Me! 'Cinco de Mayo is a holiday somewhere.'

Aw Nesta Gawd This Really Happened

Red Blood

Blood, mine or anyone else's, has always scared the hell out of me. When my own kids were little, my wife did all the cuts, bloody noses and stuff. Call me chicken, coward, whatever.

So when the l5 year old girl ran toward me at a football game, screaming, with bright, deep red blood spurting out of her neck, I damn near died. This was not your ordinary scrape; this kid had been stuck in the jugular. I yelled at her to quit running, lie down and told another kid to apply pressure. Blood was all over the place, still squirting out between the fingers of the kid applying pressure. What I did next is kind of a blur, luckily, the EMTs showed up quickly and she didn't bleed to death - just barely. Luckily, I didn't pass out.

It had been a well behaved crowd on a beautiful Friday night for high school football. It was close game, cheerleaders, the band and a big enthusiastic crowd - the youth of America at its best. Near the end of the game, I was taking the concession money to the office, walking past the bathrooms and several picnic tables where kids were visiting. As I passed one of the tables, the screams erupted and the blood began to fly. It was total chaos, kids running, screaming and blood all over the place. Although only about twenty feet away, I had no idea what had happened, only that this one girl was badly hurt and that it probably wasn't going to be this coward who saved her life.

It seems that at this table were seated some out of town girls, who got in a verbal snit with each other over something. Quick as a flash, one pulled out a knife and stuck the one across from her in the neck. No ruckus, no warning, just stabbed her. Sliced her jugular, took her to the brink of death in a second. Suddenly, a hundred flashing lights, sirens, yellow police barricades and a real somber crowd of onlookers staring at the very obvious trail of deep red blood stains on the sidewalk. Took a peaceful, Friday night slice of Americana to the brink as well.

No getting around it, the facts were clear. One girl in critical condition, another arrested for attempted murder at a Friday night football game. My pals from the media wanted to know about gangs, if we needed better security and supervision. Security? There was a rent-a-cop at the next table. Supervision? Hell, if I'd have been any closer, she might have stabbed me. Gangs? Maybe, I didn't know these kids. The blood looked the same as everyone else's.

So what does all this mean? Is this our sleepy little town's wake up call? Are kids going to kill kids, even in the last bastions of Americana? Is this happening in Chickencraw, Nebraska? Do I need to really get used to the sight of kids' bright, red blood? I can handle red wine. Maybe I should I pursue a career in the wine business? Maybe a wino?

Excuse Me! 'My brother is wearing my shoes.'

91

Aw Nesta Gawd This Really Happened

Volleyball Shorts

"If the light's just right, you can see their vaginas." That was Earl's opening line after he had motioned me into the gym lobby during the frosh volleyball game. He was a straight arrow who had been in local law enforcement for 30 years before retiring. Sensing he was serious, I didn't know what to say, so I said something dumb like,"Boy, you've got better eyesight than me, Earl." His granddaughter was on our team.

He went on to say that it was the spandex shorts they wear, "You can see everything, they're provocative as hell. There're 46 registered sex offenders in this county and I know what turns 'em on." I guess he'd interviewed some when he was a cop. At least I hope that's how he knows.

I told him that all teams wore those shorts, except the ones that wore those 'butt huggers,' which must be real special if you're one of Earl's sex offenders. I had never gotten a complaint, but did respect his opinion. I couldn't just suggest he shut up and keep his eyes on the ball, since he was a long time supporter of the school and obviously knew more about perverts than me. We had a friendly chat for about thirty minutes, but I could tell not much of what I was saying made much sense to him.

Finally, I used the old standard principal line to end a conversation. "Earl, what would you like me to do?" He wanted me to talk with the coach and get back to him. I went back into the gym, looking for the head coach. I hate to admit that for the first time ever, I was looking at those shorts and what was in them. I saw nothing but nice looking young rear ends. Honest. I finally spotted the varsity coach.

Kim is a tall, attractive, athletic, assertive and very successful volleyball coach, a great role model for young women. I told her about Earl's observations, along with his diagnostic evaluation of the local 46 sex offenders. Common decency prevents me from writing Kim's response. Some of it had to do with male anatomy and the wrestling and swim uniforms boys wear. Suffice to say, she did not agree with his assessment.

The next day, I attended an athletic league meeting. I asked all of the principals and athletic directors gathered there if they had ever had a complaint or had any concerns about volleyball uniforms. I asked the question and they waited for the punch line. They thought it was one of my dumb jokes. They were very curious to know exactly why I was asking this question.

I then asked our school psychologist about sex offenders and what turns them on. Those guys have problems that are weird and complex. She told me more than I wanted to know, but never mentioned volleyball shorts or anything close. I headed back to my office and wrote Earl a nice letter, telling him of my work exploring his concern. I mentioned that no one else seemed to be fired up and suggesting a ban on the shorts was not a crusade I chose to mount at this time. I thanked him for his continued interest and support. Taking Earl's advice, I'm going to watch for perverts at our next match. I'm also going to keep one eye on Earl, since he may have x-ray vision or something.

Excuse Me! 'I had an appointment with my personal trainer.'

Aw Nesta Gawd This Really Happened

Wally

My wife has the cutest cocker spaniel. He's a purebred with beautiful blonde fur, friendly, eager to please and if dogs could smile, he'd have a grin on his face every time you looked at him. He's probably not too bright, since he's impossible to train and we can only teach him a few tricks.   But the way he cocks his head and gazes at you, you've just got to love him. We call him Wally.

Today Congressman Wally Herger visited our school. I am not sure why he chose our school, but he is up for re-election. We were kind of honored to lead a real live guy who knows the President around our campus. We had the maintenance guys scurry around and make sure there was no trash or graffiti within view. The vice principals were ordered to run interference and clear the way - no meatballs in the hallways, nothing weird. Let's give Wally our best distorted view of American schools.

He had a large flock of media people following him; TV cameras, radio guys with recorders and print media types with notepads. He also had his personal photographer. I felt pretty important, even though I knew this had more to do with the election than our school - or education, for that matter.

I led him around campus. He was short, immaculately dressed in a dark suit, shoes shined, hair combed and smile on. His press agent, or whatever he was, had told us he wanted to visit classrooms, see kids and stuff. I think he meant that he wanted the media guys to see him seeing kids and stuff. Anyway, off we went - Wally and I and this whole flock of scurrying idiots jockeying for position every time we paused.

As we walked from place to place, Wally and I carried on a normal conversation. He seemed like an okay guy who didn't know a whole lot about schools. He was very pleasant; told me about his high school baseball team and things. However, when we stopped, even for a second, one of the media guys jumped in and asked a question. Wally suddenly stood straight, smiled perfectly and used synchronized hand gestures. I swear he also cocked his head.

The cameras rolled and Wally responded. He got questions from the media and once in a classroom even asked for student questions. I thought the student questions were pretty good, but the answers took me by surprise. He had the same three answers which he rotated, regardless of the question. I heard them all several times; the hand gestures were even identical.

Wally was doing what it takes to get elected and he seemed to be good at it. I was amazed how he could hold an expression or gesture until the photographer could get the perfect angle on Wally talking to a wheelchair bound student or whatever. He must have been easier to train than my wife's Wally.

I like both Wallys about the same. Nice guys. One runs in with the paper; the other is on the front page.

Excuse Me! 'I couldn't find anyone to baby sit my new puppy.'

93

Aw Nesta Gawd This Really Happened

Train Me

I do get confused rather easily, but it seems to me that a Youth Job Training Program would be a program to train youth for jobs. We have one of these state funded programs on our campus during the summer, and all summer I've been trying to figure out what kind of jobs these youths are being trained to do. It's the program title that confuses me the most. If it's a 'Keep 'Em Off the Streets Program,' let's call it that.

On their 'job, ' they don't show up on time, look real scruffy and move very, very slowly. I never had a job where they paid you to do that. I don't know of a job where you wouldn't get fired if you did that. They appear comatose. Their breaks are hourly and are extremely important. On the hour, they come to life and can get downright grumpy and rude if the Coke machine isn't working.

They have meetings where they get paid to plan what jobs they are going to do. A recent example was the fountain. There's this old dilapidated, non-functional drinking fountain on campus. It probably looked good fifty years ago. Fixing it is not a bad idea. The job training guys spent two days drawing plans for the renovation. The drawings were detailed and elaborate, pretty good freehand drawings.   There were cascading streams, waterfalls and gazebos. They submitted the plans to the coordinator and then proceeded to do a little pick and shovel concrete work. There's a nice little drinking fountain there now. It took 14 of them three weeks. I asked about the process. The drawings were designed to get them to 'buy in.'   Stupid me thought paying them might be 'buy in' enough. There are not many entry level construction jobs where you start out as the project architect. Oh, well.

They also had a project near the baseball field, cleaning the weeds off a side hill. I don't know if they did drawings for this project, but they did have meetings. Again, there are 14 of them. They had five rakes, five hoes and one weed eater. So ten did slow motion hoeing, raking and leaning, while the other four watched the coordinator operate the weed eater.   It seems that state law prohibits minors from running equipment, which is probably just as well. Their sagging pants make it hard enough for them to walk, let alone run something with moving parts.

I fired one of the rake leaning trainees for calling a summer school teacher a 'fucker.' He and his mother were upset with me, since this was "a training program where kids make mistakes and learn." Stupid me thought he (and the others) had finally learned a real job training lesson. The other facet I found amusing was that some of the kids quit before the summer project ended. Some were Hispanic and they could make twice as much money working with their parents in the fields, where the harder you work, the more you get paid. I don't think they do drawings out there.

So, what are they being trained to do? The training can't be for work in the real world - at least not as I know it. The 14 do have a coordinator, assistant coordinator, an aide and clerical support.   Honest. It must be job training to be job trainers.

Excuse Me! 'My uncle's nuts fell. We had to get them to the dryer.'

Aw Nesta Gawd This Really Happened

Nice Guys

"We're going to kick butt!"   Stuff like that is what Rick's basketball teams say when they charge onto the court. They always play real hard and with a lot of emotion. They are well disciplined, but no one would ever describe the way they play defense as being 'nice.' There are *never* cheap shots, but they are *fiercely* aggressive. Rick, as coach, has never won any sportsmanship awards from the officials association.

His players reflect his strong belief that a basketball game rivals World War II as a historical event in modern history. I learned this up close and personal when I accompanied the team for several years to the early season Redwood Empire Invitational Basketball Tourney.

As a van driver and the only other adult, I served as driver, chaperone, assistant coach and whatever else suited the head coach's fancy. Taking my cues from Rick, I put on a game face. That means no smiling, no joking and very little talking, just mean scowls where we all pretend we're real focused on the upcoming battle. One year was different, and I'm not sure the coach has recovered to this day.

As usual, the pre-game ritual began in earnest upon arrival at the motel. These guys should have been psyching themselves up, getting real mean and nasty. Rick had complained that these kids were talented but just too damned nice to beat anybody. We should have known they were different when three of them came running to our room soon after we checked in. They were bringing us the complimentary wine from all of the rooms because they didn't want to get in any trouble.

Rick told them they did the right thing and then snarled that they needed to get back to their rooms and get mentally prepared. Away they ran, almost skipping. He was always popular and trusted by his players and they would play hard for him. He took great pride in being able to transform regular kids into a tough unit on game day. But I think the coach sensed this group might lack the killer instinct.

Right before leaving for the gym and our first game, Rick assembled the team. We heard about focus, intensity and sacrificing your body. He covered all the details; walking into the gym with character, dressing, playing our hardest, returning to the motel, early to sleep and back at them the next day.

Now all coaches probably say this kind of stuff to their teams and then hope like hell that they don't sneak out of their rooms, drink or do other stupid things for most of the night. Most kids listen and then try to figure out the loopholes in the coach's plan. Rick ended his speech, hands on hips, with his game face firmly set by snarling "Any questions?" Much to his horror, the 6'4", 240 pound center meekly raised his hand and inquired, "Coach, do you think we could have some warm cocoa in the morning?"

The first team we played was not very good. We were ahead by a lousy point at halftime, over a team that was clearly inferior. The coach was not happy. Our guys had been real polite, quite timid - almost gracious. They smiled at the officials, helped opponents off the floor and let the other guys get most rebounds and loose balls.

I sensed that halftime was going to be interesting. The good coach went crazy. I walked in with the score book just as the first folding chair flew across the small room. His face was bright red and he was screaming that they were a number of colorful words, "pussies" being one of the milder ones I remember. He broke chalk, threw his clipboard and kicked a few more chairs. The team was deathly quiet and quite attentive.

He talked about pride, commitment, focus and effort. He challenged their manhood. He was passionate. To me, this performance had to be right up there with anything Knute Rockne ever did. I was fired up and he wasn't even talking to me.

Rick ended the performance by heading out the door and back to the gym with big, fast steps. He never looked back. His players looked at each other and then took quick, little running steps trying to catch up. I watched them all leave. I was going to pick up some of the scattered equipment, when three of them came running back in and straigtened up all of the chairs. I sensed that this was not a good sign.

We were even nicer the second half, losing by a couple of points. Our guys looked very sincere when they shook hands and congratulated the winners after the game. Rick did not go into the locker room after the game for quite a while. When he did, he talked in a soft, hoarse voice, more drained and tired than any of his players.

Later that night (in fact, a lot later), the coach and I discussed the team for some time at the B and B Lounge. How could these damn kids be so nice? What could he possibly do to make them mean and nasty? If only they weren't such good kids. We left the B and B at closing time, just in time to see a carload of winners go zooming by. We got back to the motel and players and cheerleaders from other schools were in and out of rooms and all over the place. They were splashing in and out of the motel hot tub. Their coaches were borderline neurotic.

A room check found each of our players sound asleep, presumably waiting for that cup of hot cocoa. It turned out to be a very nice season. Next year, I hope Rick gets some real jerks - or at least I think I do.

"They say that some of my stars drink whiskey. But I have found that the ones who drink milkshakes don't win many ball games."

- Casey Stengel

Excuse Me! 'It was Barry Bonds' fault. He hit a homerun and the Giants' game went into extra innings and we got home real late.'

JOE—

I HAD SUPERVISION AT LAST NIGHT'S GRADUATION
I AM AN ART TEACHER; WRITING IS NOT MY
THING! THIS DRAWING EXPRESSES MY THOUGHTS
ON THE RENT-A-COPS WE HIRE.

WES

CAN YOU DESCRIBE THE TWO WITH ALCOHOL?

Aw Nesta Gawd This Really Happened

The Show Must Go On

People in the performing arts are some of the most wonderful people I have ever met. They are creative, sensitive, tireless workers and fun to be around. Never mind that they routinely break innumerable federal edicts, state laws and district policies all in the name of the arts. They live by the poster on the band room wall - SPIT HAPPENS.

You've got to wonder how they survive. At the very least, they have little angels on their shoulders. They can easily forget a detail like requesting a bus to get the band back home from the big parade in Chico. And then just as easily have the band hitch a ride on a neighboring school's bus. They are oblivious to the convulsions of the fire marshal, school board, custodian or principal because '*the show must go on.*'

I have been privileged to have worked with some very notable - in all respects - performing arts teachers. And if they weren't exciting enough in their own right, they inspire and entice the extraordinary from their students as well. This includes all of the off the wall behavior that seems is a prerequisite to unleashing talent. All night rehearsals, power failures, fainting vocalists and minor fires are the norm. They redefine what is normal. I've been backstage while the director gives last minute instructions to the pop/jazz group, while the lead singer is throwing up in a paper bag. The retching was distracting, but the others were paying attention. But what do I know? Five minutes later the lights are on, the curtain's up and they dazzle the audience.

I have been sitting in my office on the day *Camelot* was set to open when about a dozen frantic and hysterical teenage performers stormed through my door. Through the tears and squeals, I clearly heard that King Arthur had run away from home and school. Seems the pressure had gotten to him and he was gone with about six hours till show time. They all charged out of my office wailing about suicide and worse. King Arthur indeed showed up that night, and I thought he did a pretty good job.

There was the time the dog from *Annie* took off from the set during rehearsal. They had gotten this mutt out of the pound because he had just the right look. It was the first purchase order I'd ever signed for a rabies shot and dog license. Seems he was a bit skittish, ran out of the theater when someone dropped a set and headed out across the neighborhood - at 12:30 A.M. Twenty teenagers pursued him at full speed, running across lawns, jumping fences and scaring the hell out of a significant part of the town. They never caught the dog, but believe it or not, the damn mutt showed up on the director's front porch the next morning. Annie then kept him on a leash.

It was also during *Annie* that the set became a real Hooverville. Rehearsals were running late, some of the kids didn't have rides, whatever. Yes, I was surprised, but not shocked, at eight in the morning to find a tent pitched on stage in front of Daddy Warbuck's mansion. The rest of the set was littered with clothing, sleeping bags and drowsy, ruffled teenagers. Parent permission slips, supervision - oh silly me. Seemed like the right thing to do, they said. *The show must go on.*

Excuse Me! 'It was the first week of turkey season.'

A Really Important (And Quite Rare) Letter of Recommendation

December 12, 1989

Dear Mr. Pelanconi,

Thank you for writing the letters of recommendation for me. Your praise was overwhelming, and I feel that the only way I can explain how I felt while reading them is to write a letter about you. Mr. Pelanconi's ability as a principal is only bettered by his caring for the students of his school. If there is a need at Red Bluff High School Mr. Pelanconi knows about it, for his direct interaction with the student body is so great that he knows everything that goes on at the campus. Be it talking with a member of student government or wandering through the halls at lunch, Mr. Pelanconi is always in direct contact with the students.

Mr Pelanconi is a role model for the students as well. To see the principal of a school picking up trash in the halls creates a sense of school pride that would not exist otherwise. To know that all you have to do is call his name when he walks by and he will turn and listen makes you feel important, and when he calls you by name you feel even more important.

Mr. Pelanconi place the students of his school at the top of the list, and if there is a project that needs to be done he will see to it that it is finished. What other principal would spend money out of his account to fund a student leadership program for over two hundred students at the school.

Thank you again for writing the letter of recommendation for me, but more importantly thank you for making my past four years at Red Bluff fun and challenging.

I have enclosed a book that I hope you will enjoy. Have a happy holiday season.

Sincerely,

Aw Nesta Gawd This Really Happened

Taxing Times

He charged into my office without an appointment, wagging his finger and beating his gums. I had an inkling I was not going to enjoy this conference when his opening line was "I'm a taxpayer and you work for me."

He was real angry and from what was coming out of his mouth, I wasn't sure why. Just for the record, he got no argument from me about him being a taxpayer. If he wanted to be my boss, I told him to just get in line. I was not calming him down.

His first very loud question was "What constitutional authority allows you to impose a double tax?" My answer, which was, "Huh?," just pissed him off more. He followed it with "The $5 parking permit fee is illegal; what constitutional body gave the authority to assess it?" I said, "Student council." "I demand to see the election results, I want the student council advisor's home phone number," he barked. "I don't know the exact results and I can't give you staff home phone numbers," I said.

"Remember, you work for me, so does the advisor. You illegally got my phone number from my son. I want the information now," he demanded. I just looked at him. This did not make him happy. "Answer my questions, I pay taxes! Tow my kid's car and I'll have your ass," he bellowed. I was trying to think of something to say when he followed with, "Do you idiots have bureaucrat conventions where you dream up ways to screw taxpayers and erode constitutional rights?"

Before I could say that we do have administrator conferences, but we don't call them bureaucrat conventions, he went off again. "What do you do with the illegal fee money? Pay administrator salaries?" "No, " I said. "The money goes to manage the parking program." That was not a good answer. "Manage, manage, that's bureaucratic bullshit - I knew it went to pay your salary," he roared.

This was not going well, so I thanked him for sharing and told him our little talk was over. He yelled, "Are you kicking me out of your office? I pay taxes." "No," I said. "You do pay taxes. You can sit right here as long as you want, but I'm leaving. Enjoy your stay." I then walked out of the office and closed the door behind me. A short time later, he opened the door, walked out, slammed it and left.

He wrote a letter to the Superintendent, mentioning my rudeness along with a litany of confusing constitutional points. It was a long time before he revisited my (our?) office. The next one had to do with us having an abridged version of the US Constitution in our library. I assured him that if we did, in fact, have this bad book in our library, that it was definitely not me who abridged it. He was not amused. He called me a "smart ass bureaucrat."

Our second meeting ended about the same as the first, although this time I had learned a few things about the local militia and the right to bear arms. He left before me this time. It was right after I asked him what he thought about the right to arm bears.

Excuse Me! 'Nick can't go to school cause he's sick. He can't talk to you right now cause he went down town to get some car parts.'

Principal Thoughts *Bluffer*

My '41 Buick

I've got to tell you about my old '41 Buick. I learned so much from that ugly vehicle and it's still a source of inspiration for me. But first . . .

Everyone seems to grumble about American schools. There's a lot of talk about reform and restructuring, but few people seem to understand why we're doing all this. The other day a guy told me the only reform we need is to change back to the way schools were when he was a kid.

My own daughters attended high school just a few years ago. They took all the regular courses - the very same courses I took 30 years before. Their teachers were better, the books were newer, but the curriculum was pretty much the same. It was like very little had changed in over a quarter century.

Which brings me back to the Buick. As high school kids, my buddy Dave and I bought our first car. It was a straight 8 cylinder, mostly black, 1941 Buick - without a doubt the biggest, ugliest car ever made. We walked into the junkyard, paid $40 cash, signed a few papers and became the proud owners of a small tank. Dave, being real slick on these matters, asked the seller about our warranty. He told us straight out that it had his standard 60/10 warranty - 60 seconds or 10 feet. We drove off, scrounged up $2 and bought half a tank of gas.

Dave and I loved that car. Just because we were curious, we spent most of our free time tearing that Buick apart. We knew everything about that junker. Since his father wasn't too keen on us using his tools, we dismantled and reassembled the thing with a screwdriver and crescent wrench. Amazingly, it always ran again, even when we had parts left over.

Dave's family had a ranch and a big diesel tank for the equipment. Gas was real cheap then, but his diesel was even cheaper. Besides, it was sorta neat to cruise through the small town billowing black smoke out the exhaust. We could cruise Main several times and you couldn't see across the street. People coughed and cursed a bit, but no one got real excited.

Today I have a '92 Ford Thunderbird. I have only looked under the hood once and there was nothing in there that I understood or could even identify. It takes special tools, computers and well trained pros to change the sparkplugs. I could not find the sparkplugs when I looked. Honest.

In thirty years, automobiles (and everything else) have changed at a frightening pace. Gasoline is no longer 23 cents a gallon and they'd lock up kids that smoked out a town with diesel exhaust. Yet our schools look far too much like a '41 Buick.

So that is why RBHS is changing and also why time is of the essence. Students today need to be prepared for a very different world and the old system is not going to get it done. With Career Pathways, more business involvement, community classrooms, special academies, we are designing some very different curriculums for the 21st century.

Nostalgia is great, but there just aren't many '41 Buicks left to work on.

Excuse Me! 'Our car is old and usually dead in the morning.'

Aw Nesta Gawd This Really Happened

Honk

I pass Bus 46 every morning on the way to school; it's big, yellow and crowded with active, hormonally enriched high school kids. Some mornings a kid or two will notice that the principal drove by and acknowledge me with a semi-automatic hand gesture. Most days, they are all too busy talking and poking each other for any to notice.

On this morning, I observed some extra excitement in the back seat as I approached. They were laughing, jumping around and doing things that normally irritate bus drivers. Some of the cars passing the bus in the left lane were waving and others were honking. These were obvious responses to several ninth grade cherubs holding up a hand made sign.

About the same time that I got close enough to the bus to read the rustic 'HONK IF YOU'RE HORNY' sign, one of the binder paper artists recognized me. As if on cue, the last three rows of the bus dove to the floorboard. I could see the confused bus driver barking commands as she craned her neck while looking into the huge rear view mirror over the visor. I was rather proud that the apostrophe in 'YOU'RE' and all else appeared to be grammatically correct.

I honked and drove on by.

Whatever Works

A Red Bluff Bluff

Many seniors turn 18 during their senior year. Some choose to abuse the rights and privileges that go with being a full-fledged adult. The Bluff goes something like this:

"I've got some good news and some bad news, Bill. The good news is you're now a grown man. You make your own decisions, write your own notes and are not subject to any of those silly compulsory attendance laws. There is nothing I can do to you if you choose to continue to not attend school regularly. Welcome to the adult world.

The bad news is that I just dropped you from school. Please don't let the door hit you in the rear on your way out."

The response is usually something like this:

"But that isn't fair. It's not my fault I turned 18. I'm the same as I was before. I just had a birthday was all. I'm still a kid. . . my dad'll kill me. Can I sign something and promise to attend all the time?"
"Well, let's make a deal."

Excuse Me! 'Someone stole my skateboard and I had no transportation.'

Aw Nesta Gawd This Really Happened

Realignment

If you look at a map of the Middle East, sit down and use a little logic, you can come up with what appears to be a solution to the border strife, Palestinian homeland question and most everything else. Why have wars? It isn't that complicated. Let's all be reasonable.

Oh, but only if it were that simple. The hassles and hatred go back to Biblical times. There is no logic. Athletic league realignment at the high school level is about the same. I know, because I was stupid enough to be chairman of the Section's realignment committee.

The Northern Section has seventy or so high schools scattered over an area a whole lot bigger than many Third World countries. Hayfork is a small school and a summer's vacation from anywhere, Yreka is a sorta big school near the Oregon border, Lassen is similar and closer to Reno than anywhere else and Quincy is a medium sized school up in the mountains surrounded by tiny, vocal schools. Rio Vista and Delta are south of Sacramento and somehow pretend they are a lot closer. Like little mushrooms, Christian schools seem to pop up and disappear everywhere. The rest are kinda scattered around randomly in a large valley and two mountain ranges. They range in size from about 20 students to 2000.

Now it would be nice if we could move the really far-away schools a little closer to civilization. However, that's not likely, even though it might be simpler. And wouldn't it be swell if all seventy something schools hadn't had to cut their athletic travel budgets for the forty-third straight year. It would also be convenient if enrollments stayed the same and there were never new schools or the need for change. It's also safe to say no one will ever want to go to Hayfork except for a summer vacation.

So there's this realignment committee, a representative from each of the ten leagues and the dufus chairman, me. A nice enough group of people, the committee is charged with making things fair by considering geography, enrollment and competitive strength. There are open meetings and the members listen - and listen. There are dozens of proposals and none of them include Hayfork. Finally, after months, the committee concludes that there is no simple solution. It then makes a recommendation and ducks.

It took me awhile, but I finally figured out that logic and fairness are not necessary considerations. The trick is to come up with something that irritates everyone a little bit and doesn't piss off any one school big time. Something like "Yeah, you're going to Yreka, but certainly not Lassen, too, and you won't ever have to worry about Hayfork."

That strategy helps keep the lawyers out of it, although the newspaper guys seem to have a field day no matter what happens. In fact, these print media guys seem so astute, I would suggest that we let them do realignment. Let them meet and figure it out, while we sit around taking shots at them. Oh, but I digress. . .

Now the most interesting part of the process is the impassioned pleas by individual schools. They range from tear jerking testimonials designed to put a lump in your throat to high tech presentations with maps, won/loss records, mileage charts and enrollment projections. Occasionally it's a terse and direct demand like "We won't go to Hayfork." Most are presented by the school's principal, who has been sent into the snake pit by his superintendent, board, coaches and alumni.

If you take out the emotion, some of the proposals include some downright ludicrous and humorous thoughts. Like the private Catholic school whose presentation was simply "Our old bus won't make it to Hayfork." Okay. Which prompted me to irreverently ask, "Where's the Pope when you need him?"

Or the side by side, same size schools in the same district who, for reasons unknown to me, requested to *not* be in the same league. Or the three rather close valley schools, who whined incessantly about being separated and put in a more logical configuration. Not at all unlike the Palestinian homeland, their tradition, they whined, goes back to Biblical times.

There's safety issues, you know. Flatlander bus drivers can't drive in the mountains. Leagues need similar schedules. The mountain schools have to finish football season before the snow flies, while the flatlanders would have you believe that every football player picks fruit till there's frost on the pumpkin.

Then there was also the 35 student (projected!) Christian school in Hayfork, of all places. They planned to be an athletic power and wanted in a league. This was conveniently solved when the principal/presenter was arrested for molestation and the school folded.

But my all time favorite was the valley school that wanted into a smaller league because many of its students were Hmong. The principal made an articulate and impassioned plea that those Southeast Asians shouldn't be counted in enrollment tallies because they don't like athletics. While listening to this one, I couldn't help but wonder if this guy thought other schools should have to count Blacks twice, since a racist might say that they really like athletics. It also seemed very interesting to me that today's paper lists a kid named Thong Yang as this same school's leading scorer. What?

Amazingly, after hundreds of faxes and phone calls, volumes of paper and a ton of hot air, the process ground to a conclusion. Luckily, and perhaps a tribute to my skill as an irritant, everyone was unhappy. Hayfork was probably the only school that didn't grumble and that was because they were too far away to attend the meeting.

Hey, but no one was going crazy. At least for awhile, there was going to be no lawyers, no Holy War. As I understand it, Jerusalem is a lot like Hayfork in reverse. I wonder if I could help out those Arabs and Jews.

Excuse Me! 'We went deer hunting way up by Hayfork and my dad's 4 wheel drive Jeep broke an axle. We had to hike out of this big honkin' canyon.'

This Is a Crackers Job

What Works For Me

There is nothing that can prepare a person to be a high school principal. It is an exciting microcosm of everything that is happening in the real world. That in itself can be a scary thought if you ponder it for even a few seconds. It comes at you from all directions and whatever is written in your daily planner become suggestions, at best. However, there are a few characteristics (quirks?) that I think are critical to survive in what is a uniquely American job.

I've decided that a short attention span is the greatest asset a high school principal can possess. Couple it with appropriate proportions of nervous energy, risk taking and impulsiveness and you have a personality that may not be driven totally crazy by the kaleidoscope job. Ironically, those same characteristics have appeared on more than a few special ed referrals. Oh well. . . . .

Add to these traits a healthy sense of humor and you've got a chance. Taking oneself or what one does too seriously can be fatal. It's a matter of listening, grinning, dealing with it and moving on. That's what works for me. To do it any other way would take a much smarter person than me.

Which reminds me of the day a well dressed, articulate mother asked to speak to the School Board about our spring musical. Her daughter had a small part as a Chinese coolie in *Anything Goes*. They were of Asian descent and it was pretty ugly stereotypical casting. I was ready to apologize profusely for our racial insensitivity. Wrong!!

She delivered a well prepared monologue at the Board meeting on the anti-Christian and pornographic script and how this Cole Porter classic was ill-suited for high school students. She was particularly offended by the antics of the inebriated preacher in the cast. I had thought his part was quite humorous and that the musical had been done in pretty good taste. It wasn't *Hair*, but what do I know?

The lady continued with her perfect diction, soft voice and wonderfully serene smile. If anyone has Jesus in their heart, this woman surely did. She ended her presentation with a plea to change our direction in the interest of our children's safety and welfare. It was the role of parents to address these issues. Didn't we care that we were losing a whole generation to Satan?

The less organized and more emotional supporters who followed her to the podium admitted that they had not seen the musical, but demanded that we root Satan out of our schools. *Anything Goes,* along with sex education, were examples of the poisoning of children's minds by secular and insensitive educators. Many church and community members shared their values. They vowed to be back. I vowed to keep my mouth shut and not verbally respond.

The next morning I sat in my office wondering how to answer a concerned parent who had caught me completely off guard, yet deserved a written response. Man, these people were going to be real fired up if they ever find out we do Shakespeare, Twain, Steinbeck and all those weirdos. Nothing was coming to me; I was beginning to grin and my attention span was waning. My secretary then told me another mother and daughter were here to see me. Send 'em in.

Gina was real opinionated, but generally a pleasant girl and a good student. I had never met her mother. They came in with a newspaper clipping telling of the Marin County high school dispersing condoms on campus. Gina did most of the talking. They were both serious and intense. They wanted to know why we had no similar program.

More specifically, they referred to our "Neanderthal awareness and polyanna approach" to serious problems. With AIDS, teenage pregnancy and all the rest we absolutely had to get involved. Parents weren't doing the job and our sex education program barely scratched the surface, so to speak. I listened to all of the events leading up to and following Gina's miscarriage. It was a touching story, but they could have spared me the gory details.

Weren't we concerned with children's safety and welfare? Why must we keep our heads in the sand? "A Red Bluff Cracker mentality," they called it. They thought maybe a petition or trek to the School Board might get me moving. They emphasized that many members of the community shared their values. They vowed to be back. Although I wanted to explain I had nothing to do with Gina's pregnancy and also thought AIDS was a terrible disease, I vowed to keep my mouth shut and hear them out.

What if Gina and her mom had showed up at last night's Board meeting? That could have been a real exciting event. But again, my mind was wandering and I was beginning to get confused on who complained about what. Who was worried about safety and welfare? Which ones had a lot of community support? Parents? Values? I was beginning to grin and lose my focus.

I needed to get a hold of myself and do my job, so I dutifully and impulsively wrote them similar responses. I thanked them for sharing and caring. I assured them that we would take their suggestions very seriously and that I would be pleased to talk with them if they had further questions. Blah, blah, blah. The fact was that I took neither of them very seriously and hoped I'd never see either of them again.

No sooner had I finished the letters when my secretary told me a football player and father wanted to see me. Now, could this be a man seeking equal access to football for his handicapped son (daughter!)? Or maybe a dad wanting me to change a star quarterback's grade so he wouldn't be in the grandstand Friday night? Condoms in the locker room? Prayers before the game?

It didn't matter. I looked forward to seeing them; it would get my mind off the others and who had been complaining about something, the details of which were becoming fuzzy.

Can you imagine what a living hell it would be to anyone who remembered, pondered and worried about all this stuff? Or how devastating it would be to take any of it very seriously? Thank goodness (let's leave God out of this!) for my sense of humor and short attention span. It is what works for me.

Excuse Me! 'I had to stay home to see John's execution on Days of Our Lives.'

Principal Thoughts *Bluffer*

SAT

This is the time of the year when students, especially seniors, start talking about their SATs. Now, everyone knows that SATs are numbers that are sent to students from the mysterious Educational Testing Service in Princeton, New Jersey. Nobody seems to have the vaguest idea how this ritual got started or if it has much to do with the real world. Nonetheless, most agree it's a big deal.

SAT actually stands for Scholastic Aptitude Test, whose results are required by most universities and colleges for admission. This is not to be confused with the PSAT, which is sort of the junior varsity version of the test and it doesn't count. We take the PSAT to let us know what we are in for, increase our anxiety and get practice in sharpening number two pencils.

Everyone also knows that how these SAT numbers are arranged has a great deal to do with what college wants you and if anyone is willing to give you big money to go there. For example, SAT numbers like 1450 are much better than 0541. This can be the difference between free books and tuition at Stanford and paying your own way to the college I went to.

The SAT numbers (scores) are the result of a whole room full of students, strategically seated at safe distances. They are all staring blankly, while squeezing number 2 lead pencils in their sweaty hands. They are trying to answer hundreds of questions for which there appears to be no right answer. These are questions like "RED BLUFF is to HEAVEN as ANDERSON is to _____." You then get four multiple choices, none of which seems like the perfect answer.

In all my years in education, I have never heard anyone leaving the test say something like, "that quiz was sure a piece of cake," although we did once have a student who got a perfect 800 on the math portion of the SAT. They paid him to go to Stanford, by the way. Most of us, however, leave the test demoralized and not real sure if we got any answers correct.

Sometimes all of this seems a bit unfair. Some mysterious beings, somewhere in New Jersey, are sending us these numbers that greatly affect our future. While better students tend to have higher scores, no one is even certain the scores relate to much of anything except maybe native intelligence and test taking skills.

In fact, as a result of recent criticism, those phantom folks in New Jersey changed the SAT exam. From what I've read, the changes will make the test a more accurate measure of how we will perform in college. Parts of the test will now have us demonstrate what we can actually do. This is good news, since it will now relate a bit more to what we teach in school.

Regardless of what we think of the SAT or those folks somewhere in New Jersey, the test appears to be here to stay in one form or another. Consequently, it behooves us to try and figure out the rules of the game and be as prepared as possible. Red Bluff grads do well in college and we need to make sure they have the right numbers to get there.

Encouraging students to work hard and do well in challenging classes is one obvious strategy. Another is to review test-taking skills with our counselors. They can help us to become familiar with the computer software and printed material we have to share with you. We can win the SAT game - and a game it is.

After all, KNOWLEDGE is to FUTURE as SAT is to _____; a) AGONY, b) INSANITY, c) SUICIDE, d) OPPORTUNITY.

Teenagers Are People Too!

Excuse Me! 'My brain was fatigued.'

Thoughts While Eating Pasta

Principally Italian

I'm Italian. I'm sorry. I can't help it. I was born that way. I grew up that way. Like all wops, family is everything to me. God knows, from Mama to Mafia, family defines us. Don't mess with family. We do real stupid things defending family. I'm an Italian principal, or more accurately, principally Italian. Kids in my school are family. So is the staff who takes care of them. All educators say kids are top priority. However, ed codes, county offices, policies, district offices, contracts, unions and good ol' boys always seem to come first when the rubber hits the road.

Rules and bureaucrats are not family. A principal, who's principally Italian, owes them nothing. If it's not good for kids, it's not good. Knowing what is good or bad for kids is as simple as the difference between red wine and red wine vinegar. One makes you smile; the other makes you pucker. Ignoring stupid rules makes me smile. Irritating stupid bureaucrats is fun. "Nice rule. It's not good for my family. What's the penalty?"

I am not opposed to smiling, talking fast and employing a little sleight of hand to get around obstacles. That's sometimes easier, but facing the consequences is not painful; it is a duty - almost an honor. What appears to be a reckless risk to others is perfectly normal to me. This explains why no one has ever begged me to "move on up," as they say. In fact, I am certain that many are amazed that I wasn't fired years ago. Quite honestly, so am I. It would be the ultimate honor to be fired defending family against the absurd and often destructive rules, memos and morons that routinely bombard a principal from Sacramento and other encampments a lot closer to home.

Which leads me to three days of uncharacteristic self restraint on my part, as well as pathetic concession to absurd bureaucratic nonsense. We have just been WASCed. The seven accreditation evaluators arrived the day after 40 Italian students and teachers had spent three weeks with us. My previous experience with WASC had been painless, but these folks, with rules in hand, were clueless. Combined with three weeks of Italian logic, their visit was torturous. If these WASCers had ever talked with a teen, any teen, they concealed it well. They said we have a good school, but "We just can't figure it out" and "You don't follow the rules." Everyone seemed so happy, teachers were teaching, there was evidence students were learning, but "How does it work?" Obviously, none had ever been to Italy. They kept looking at their checklists and asking who was was responsible for this or that and the "We all are" answers just did not compute.

Luckily, we had staff who could dazzle them with data. I bit my tongue and they checked all the right boxes. I wished I'd have told them it's not about flow charts; it's about family. If you care about kids, work hard and do the right thing, it all works out. Another part wishes I'd have told them to take their forms, assessments, rules and strategic plans and shove them where the sun doesn't shine.

In the end, with a glowing evaluation in hand, I feel a bit dishonest and dirty. So?

Excuse Me! 'John was late for school because he is too damn slow.'

Stupidest Questions Asked By Parents and the Answer
I Didn't Give

Question: I strongly oppose your sex education program. It goes against all of our religious beliefs. Do you have a background in psychology and secular humanism?
Answer: Yes, in fact, I have. It was in a psych class where I first met Jimmy Swaggart and first got into sexual perversion and sex education.

Question: Can't you just teach my kid to read and write and can the Shakespeare crap?
Answer: The lady doth protest too much, methinks. *Hamlet Line 242*

Question: I've always taught my kid to stand up for his rights. Why did you suspend him for fighting?
Answer: You got a point there, Rambo. We are considering having our School Board members quit voting on issues - just duke it out.

Question: Michael tried real hard this year; brought his grades up and was hardly in any trouble. Why didn't he get a community scholarship?
Answer: After careful consideration of transcripts, records and tests, the scholarship committee unanimously agreed that your son is stupid as a post, and beyond that, they concluded that he remains an absolute jerk.

Question: All things considered, my daughter is handling having her picture left out of the yearbook very well. I was Miss Ventura County, you know, and I would have been devastated. How could you have done this?
Answer: If, in a previous life, you indeed were Miss Ventura County, I'll bet you showed up for the pageant. Your little princess cut school on picture day and again on the makeup day.

Question: Can you explain why my son, who is gifted, should have to be in classes with students of average ability?
Answer: Well, I must tell you that your son's teachers wholeheartedly agree. They would all like that arrogant, self centered little snot to be most anywhere else.

Question: Your teachers are heathens, your students barbarians and I'm transferring my daughter to a private church school. What do you have to say about that?
Answer: Please allow me to help with the tuition.

"This isn't right. This isn't wrong.
This is just plain stupid."
- Mickey Bitsko

Excuse Me! 'My horse was sick and he needed me.'

Aw Nesta Gawd This Really Happened

Principal Pipsqueak

No one has ever accused me of being a hulking or intimidating presence, but until this Board Meeting I had never been called a Pipsqueak either. Maybe it was because this guy was bigger than me or something. Anyway, he was in a foul mood because the Board was expelling his kid and probably for a lot of other reasons that none of us really want to know about.

Junior had threatened some girls on a school bus with a hand gun. Probably not NRA members, the girls didn't notice that it was actually a plastic weapon that looked a lot like a real gun. They only knew that it scared the crap out of them and that their mothers needed to know right away. Their mothers immediately delivered the hysteria, along with an ample dose of anger, right to my office. The police were involved. Some would say it was an open and shut case. Education codes are quite clear on what you can get expelled for and, plastic or not, this gun thing was serious. We had the evidence, a toy plastic gun, in our office prior to the Board Meeting, where expulsion was being considered.

The day before the meeting Dad came by the office and insisted to the clerical staff that he had a right to the evidence, since they were going to visit the probation office. I'm no lawyer, but that didn't sound kosher to me. I had told staff he wasn't getting the gun. This did not make him happy and he became quite belligerent with staff. He said he'd been told he could have it.

Trying to get staff out of the firing line, I intervened. Furthermore, I chose to disagree with him and suggested he might not be telling the truth. Well, actually I said he was a liar, since there'd been a few other instances where he'd hassled staff and his perceptions had not been in line with most everyone else's. My choice of words was probably not a good idea, although it amused the office staff. I was afraid they might applaud. He left, pronouncing that he was a man of the gospel and not a liar.

He then appeared at the Board Meeting and asked to plead his case in open session. His defense did mention that the boy had only been kidding around with a harmless toy, but the focus of his presentation had to do with the sour attitude of Principal Pipsqueak. By his account, Pipsqueak had a vendetta against his family, called them names and was totally out of control in most situations. He thought it his duty to inform the Board of the unprofessional behavior of Principal Pipsqueak.

The Board voted to expel the boy. None of the Board members ever called me Pipsqueak, but it should be noted that the expulsion vote was not unanimous. He was later given back the gun and he had it when he went to the County School Board for the appeal. Unfortunately for him, they upheld the decision. Having the gun probably did not help his case. The County Board members flinched noticeably when this man of the gospel pulled the plastic gun out of a paper sack to demonstrate its insignificance.

Excuse Me! 'I stayed home because not one person at that school likes my mother.'

Aw Nesta Gawd This Really Happened

Mrs. Miller was a veteran teacher. She'd taught smart ones, slow ones, at risk, home study and more. She'd taught in several schools. By her own account, she'd been around and thought she'd seen it all.

At the beginning of the lunch break, she came into my office, uncharacteristically shaken. As near as I can recollect (and I recollect this one pretty well), our conversation went like this:

Mrs. M: Joe, I've been married 28 years. . . I've raised two sons. You better sit down for this one.

Me: Uh, okay.

Mrs. M: Simon Smalley is kind of a weird kid, but I've seen a lot of strange ones. He's actually been pretty normal this semester. All freshmen are a little squirrelly. Do you know him?

Me: I don't think so. What'd he do?

Mrs. M: He was the only kid in my 4th period class who didn't want to go to the assembly. He and I were the only ones in the room, me at my desk correcting papers and him in the back of the room, sitting in a chair with his back to me . . . Are you sure you don't know him? He wears that big chain hooked to his wallet.

Me: Maybe I'd recognize him if I saw him.

Mrs. M: Well, I wasn't really paying any attention to him, I was correcting papers. It's hard to keep up with all these writing assignments, you know. . . This is not easy, but I have to tell you. Anyway, I noticed out of the corner of my eye that Simon was acting weird back there. He had turned the desk toward the wall and was moving around sort of like he was listening to music or something, but he doesn't even have one of those Walkmans. , , .

Me: And?

Mrs. M: Well, I quietly got up and walked around the side of the room to see what he was doing. He was . . . I've been married 28 years, have two sons . . . he was jacking off, you know, masturbating. That's the honest truth, I swear to God.

Me: I don't think you'd make this up. What'd you do?

Mrs. M: He didn't see me. I think he had his eyes closed. I quietly hurried back to my desk before he saw me. Then when there was a break in the action, so to speak, I told him to go lunch early. He left and I'm here. This is so embarrassing, but I had to tell someone. I figured you'd know what to do. Maybe I should have called the psychologist. Maybe I should have taken him straight to the office.

Me: I don't think so. You did the right thing. I'm sorry you had to go through this. I'll find the kid.

Mrs. M: One last thing. I know I didn't do or say anything at all to, you know, turn him on. Look at me. I dress very conservatively. I'm certainly not young and attractive. The kid just had the urge, I guess. I had nothing to do with it. Honest.

Me: I am absolutely sure that's true. Please don't worry about that.

Mrs. M: Should I fill out an accident report or something?

Me: Maybe an incident report. This is a first. I'll handle it.

Mrs. M: What are you going to do with him? I don't really want to talk with his mother.

Me: Nor do I. I have no clue. I'll do something.

"Truth is stranger than fiction – to some people."

- Mark Twain

Excuse Me! 'My little brother was cutting and I was out looking for him.'

Whiners

Stuff happens. It just does. It always has. And its not always good stuff. Johnny got a lousy grade in math. Suzy broke her ankle playing basketball. There is nothing different or new here. However, what may be new is the way people handle setbacks.

This past summer I read a book by Charles Sykes, who says that America has become a nation of spoiled crybabies, whining their lives away. We expect life to be pain free, and if it's not, we blame someone else. If you lose your job, you sue your boss for mental distress or if you get drunk and run your car into a tree, you sue the bar that sold you the liquor.

If people gamble, drink, overeat, abuse, or whatever, they no longer are irresponsible, according to Sykes. They are now in need of treatment. We have support groups for everything. We often believe bad things happen to us because of prejudice. Nearly everyone is part of at least one oppressed minority group - even women - who are actually the majority. We are all victims, adopting the credo "admit nothing, blame everyone and be bitter."

For me, the Sykes book changed my thinking. I am no longer interested in a principals' support group. I'm not going to blame the teachers when the students don't like me. It is not my parents' fault that I did not attend Harvard or that I'm afraid of snakes. This guy Sykes seems to make some good sense.

All too often, I see Johnny ragging about the teacher when he gets a lousy math grade. Couldn't it be that he just chose not to do the work? Maybe he should suck it up and put in more effort. Couldn't clumsy Suzy have just flopped down and munched her ankle? Couldn't it just have been bad luck, which, after all, is better than no luck at all? Suzy's going to sue the coach, the school and the company that makes the gym floor wax. Even institutions can be victims. Some schools will tell you that Johnny can't read because "they cut the budget" or "kids nowadays are different." This may be true, but so what! Quit complaining. Just teach the meatball to read. He might sue if you don't.

The problem with this being a victim stuff and wallowing in self pity is that it prevents us from getting where we want to go. Successful people plow right through adversity, getting help when they need it, but not blaming someone else for the setbacks. Columbus would have never found the New World if he'd gone back and sued the guy that gave him the flat world map.

I can only imagine how successful our schools would be if we forgot about blaming, whining and suing and just got on with education. Like the commercial says, "Just do it!" And like my mother used to say, "Quit whining!" Everyone would be judged on their own character and be responsible for their own actions. I really doubt that Abe Lincoln spent a lot of time sniveling about the lousy textbooks and bad light in his log cabin.

"Life is just a bowl of pits."
- Rodney Dangerfield

Excuse Me! "I can't believe I had the 3 day measles for 2 weeks."

Aw Nesta Gawd This Really Happened

Chopper Homecoming

Over the years, we've done a few things right. We've had super accreditations, Fullbright teachers, Merit Scholars, state commendations. Hell, one year test scores even went up. We did press releases, had back page newspaper articles, sometimes badgered a local station for 20 second TV coverage. I don't remember anyone out there ever calling or writing to congratulate us on our competence. I don't even recall any 'attaboys.' You get used to the public appearing to not care about the things everyone says the public cares about.

Hey, but when the choppers flew into the football stadium during Homecoming, it was a whole new ball game. Phone calls, letters, e-mail. "You're a first class school." "Boy, you guys do it right." "We're so proud of our school." "Blah, blah, blah." You'da thought we landed on the moon - and I never pretended we weren't going to do that next year.

Our Homecomings had always been special, with fireworks, floats, pretty queens, sleek cars and all that. We're big on tradition. With six candidates in beautiful dresses, two MCs and lots of flowers, the town photographer's down on the field going crazy. It's SRO, with thousands in the stands. Last year's queen crowns the new one. My role is to give the MCs the envelope. I always shine my shoes and wear the tuxedo I bought at Rags to Riches for $25. In small town America, Homecoming's a fun time; a real big deal.

However, this last one was spectacular. If you've ever watched those M*A*S*H reruns, you know how the show was a raucous comedy, interspersed with bits of brutal reality. The sobering sound and sight of choppers coming over the horizon carrying a new load of wounded soldiers sticks with you.

Sitting on the field, next to the coronation stage, that M*A*S*H scene kept flashing through my mind. I swear I could hear the theme song. It was dusk, the orange sun barely over the Coast Range. You could hear them in the distance, the unmistakable chopper sound, see their blinking lights, heading right toward us, over the western goal post, in perfect formation.

For just a second, I imagined I was Alan (Hawkeye) Alda and it was Hotlips Hoolihan sitting next to me. Just like M*A*S*H, the goofy aura of Homecoming frivolity was being interrupted by an ominous, almost scary, sound coming nearer and nearer and getting louder and louder. People were noticeably confused and nervous. The next scene would cut to the M*A*S*H operating room tent, serious doctors, grimacing, bloody soldiers.

It was actually last year's queen sitting next to me, but it was one of those special moments that can do weird things to your reality. Suddenly I had become Hawkeye, looking for Klinger and Radar. I was in a weird place and I was one of only a few who knew the choppers were coming. I can only imagine what the overflow crowd, that included most of the town, thought, since they were patiently awaiting the courtly and traditional promenade down the stadium aisles.

Shiny silver and black, the three identical choppers hovered in front of a stunned crowd for a minute or two and then landed on the field in unison. They shut down the choppers and the props slowly and methodically came to a halt. The crowd was eerily silent for an elongated second or two. Then a nervous chatter erupted and lasted for another few seconds before the crowd finally broke into uproarious applause.

Dressed in black, a ground crew sprinted out of the darkness and rolled out three red carpets. The cockpit doors opened and six beautiful young women emerged, two from each helicopter. Met and escorted by their fathers, they traipsed, one by one, down the red carpet toward the grandstand. Their smiles lit up the stadium. It was spectacular. You had to be there - one of those goose bump memories.

Once emptied of their unique cargo, the choppers started their engines in unison, hovered over the field for a few seconds, tipped the chopper noses in a salute to the crowd and in perfect formation flew back out through the goal post into the western night. People expect to see this kind of stuff at the Super Bowl halftime or somewhere, not at a funky high school homecoming. The crowd was strangely euphoric. There was a weird electricity in the air. Some people even cried. The local photographer was running low on film and about to engage in some serious hyperventilation. I was over my M*A*S*H fantasy and just damn glad nothing screwed up.

High schools don't do these kinds of things. Maybe we're not even supposed to do these things. It was not our idea and we hadn't spent much time planning it. We sorta got caught up in it and, if the truth be known, I damn near wet my pants when it was suggested by the four Gunsauls Brothers. They are local grads who own a helicopter company and wanted to do something special for their alma mater. It was their show, their expense, their FAA approval, their insurance and their red carpets. They had all the right answers for the skeptical Superintendent and awe struck School Board. They swore everyone to secrecy.

Nonetheless, the Chopper Homecoming has enhanced our school's image beyond belief. We got calls of congratulations, media coverage and accolades like you wouldn't believe. A derelict we expelled last year ran up and gave me a high five during the third quarter of the game. Go figure. There's no doubt that the community thinks I'm a whole lot smarter than a few short weeks ago. Our math program is better, test scores are up, seniors are going to Harvard. The Homecoming show was so dramatic, no one even groused that our football team got pummeled during the game. That, in itself, was a first.

A small part of me says I should explain the school's minimal role with a bit more vigor. But, what the hell, we didn't always deserve the crap we've gotten at other events beyond our control, so why not just go with it? However, I never dreamed we'd get this good. It's almost embarrassing. Ah, but I blew it. I should have realized that we are not going to top this one. We really won't go to the moon next Homecoming. Test scores will never be this high again. I'm going to get stupid again. I should have grabbed Hotlips, jumped into that last helicopter and flown off into the sunset.

Excuse Me! 'Kayla stayed home to look for her dogs.'

Cindy's Note and Doug's Reply

Doug

    I want your body, You
excite me so much! I go
home every day and dream
about you then find myself
having an orgasm!

    I want you to:
Take me
hold me
use me
abuse me
whip me
beat me
eat me

    I love you forever,
      Cindy

Cindy,
I don't know how to do all that stuff.
    Doug

Principal Thoughts *Bluffer*

Mr. Blandsworth

So the principal has a Raiders' jacket. What's the big deal? Heck, I've been a Raiders' fan for years; the jacket's warm and the hood's great in the rain. For some reason, it has generated all sorts of interest. Has he joined a gang? All principals look alike; what's with ours?

I guess it rattled someone's stereotype - someone's prejudiced notion of the way principals are supposed to look. If true, that's scarey. Stereotyping is just sort of a learner's permit for things like sexism, racism, hatred and bigotry. And God knows how I hate bigots! (What?)

One of the many things I love about Red Bluff High is that people have the freedom and security to break the stereotypes which often drive teenagers (old people, too) into sick cliques. Aren't ASB presidents supposed to be preppy? Dustin wears a cowboy hat and rides bulls. Aren't cheerleaders ditsy airheads? Mandi has straight A's. Aren't football players superjocks who wouldn't be caught dead acting or singing? Aaron has a lead in Romeo and Juliet. Tyler sings in the Gold Show.

And what about the staff? Where else is there a female teacher who organizes an arm wrestling tourney? An electronics teacher with a great singing voice? Or a chemistry teacher who raises hogs and eucalyptus trees? A football coach who studies ballet? Amazingly, it goes on and on at Red Bluff High.

So, give me the same break everyone else at our school enjoys. There's already a conspiracy out there to make principals look like the biggest idiots on the planet. Just think of all those dumb TV sit coms that deal with schools and then think about how the principal looked and acted. How about "Head of the Class"? Do you remember that overweight buffoon who was the brunt of most of the jokes? They are all blatant stereotypes just like that - ugly principalism.

And it isn't just TV - the problem is much deeper than that. The brainwashing starts in preschool. My very own wife teaches preschool and one of her favorite storybooks is "Miss Nelson Is Back." A main character is Mr. Blandsworth, the principal, and boy, is he ever a classic moron. Those poor little preschoolers sit there on their rugs and are fed that garbage. No wonder they all want to be firemen, astronauts, nurses and veterinarians. Have you you ever heard one say they wanted to be a principal?

Nonetheless, I am undaunted. With your help, we can eradicate one of the last awful stereotypes on our campus. Good grief, if a football player can be Romeo, the principal should get some slack. In fact, I'm looking for just the right cowboy hat. I'll still wear a necktie and stuff, but no way am I going to be a Mr. Blandsworth look-alike.

And one more thing - if any of you turkeys call me Mr. Blandsworth, I'll get my gang after you big time!

P.S. !Hola, amigos mexicanos! No es justo que se dice que somos los mismos simplemente porque llevamos ropa negra. Cada uno es diferente en su propia manera. Podemos llegar a ser lo que queremos. Gregoria seria una buena presidenta de escuela. Ay caramba, Maurilio seria un director estupendo. !Viva la diferencia!

"I've never had much interest in being liked. I think that's what people like about me."
- Mickey Bitsko

Excuse Me! 'He's afraid of the coyotes he hears at the bus stop.'

117

Aw Nesta Gawd This Really Happened

Chastity Upbottom

Every class has at least one Chastity Upbottom in it. It must be some kind of unwritten law - a kinda gut check for principals. If you can't handle little Chastity and Mr. and Mrs. Upbottom, you're going to be back teaching geography.

There are certain unwritten rules that dictate behaviors, dress and everything else about Chastity's aura. For example, Chastity never walks to school, or, heaven forbid, rides one of those proletariat school buses. She is delivered; not to the student parking lot, but to the main office. Mrs. Upbottom usually does the honors, helping Chastity with her books and dispensing a goodbye kiss on her sweet little cheek.

The Upbottoms are not extra wealthy, but one wouldn't know it by looking at Chastity's wardrobe. There are lots of frilly dresses, designer jeans and stuff that go real well with her scrubbed complexion and perfect hairdo. Zits, grit and whatever bizarre teenage fashion fad that's in, are strictly forbidden. Few teachers dress as well.

In fact, Chastity does very well in the adult world. In class, she absolutely always says and does the right thing. Her teachers count on her to model studious righteousness and many point out her perfection to the class time and again. She will slip a note to the substitute, telling that her classmates are not sitting in their assigned seats. The class, in turn, generally hates her guts.

It is quirks like this that usually get the principal involved with the Upbottoms. Chastity usually runs for freshman class president. Her campaign posters are perfect, her dress and speech are inspiring and she loses to a boy, whose posters are a bit off color. He gives a terrible speech in cutoffs and a tank top. It's not even close; a big time blowout. Chastity is crushed.

Enter Mr. and Mrs. Upbottom for the first of many conferences where the principal listens and listens. He listens to lectures on virtue, decency, morality, hard work, fairness, to name just a few. There are many not so subtle suggestions that anyone who manages this ungodly institution must embody some pretty disgusting traits himself. All the while he listens, knowing that if he slips just once and tells them what he really thinks, it'll be back to the geography classroom. They make subtle threats and the School Board would love Chastity.

That frosh election is just the beginning. Chastity is going to volunteer to chair the Christmas sing-along at the convalescent hospital and then be the only one who shows up. She is not going to get a prom date unless she strong arms some underclassman. Some idiot is going to steal her new leather jacket. Some kid from an "average" family and questionable morals is going to Girls' State. On and on.

One must be patient and not vomit the truth. Justice will prevail. Chastity is never completely and totally perfect. Like the time Chastity just happened to get caught with the teacher's edition of her history book. I hate to admit how much I enjoyed lecturing the Upbottoms on honesty and integrity. No I don't!

Excuse Me! 'My parents ran away from home.'

More Stupid Parent Questions
And the Answers I Didn't Give

Question: My daughter's hair is blue, yes BLUE. Why do kids insist on being so rebellious?
Answer: I think its because you are far more interested in what's on top of your daughter's head, rather than inside it.

Question: It is sexist to allow only the fathers of Homecoming Queen candidates to escort their daughters. What about the mothers?
Answer: Hey, I agree. The whole queen thing smacks of meat market, female exploitation, sexist stuff. Let's get rid of it.

Question: Do you see a lot of kids who get screwed up by drugs?
Answer: I see kids who get screwed up by parents. Drugs just finish them off.

Question: My kid took my car to the Winter Formal and some idiot plowed into it during the dance. There's a car in your parking lot with blue paint on its bumper. Would you go look?
Answer: I already did. It's not there.

Question: Today is Michael's very first day of high school. Do you know if he ate his lunch?
Answer: Yes, he did – even the green beans. He also wore his sweater all day.

Question: The dance teacher said my daughter's breasts are too large to be on the dance team. Do you have a policy on this?
Answer: Just how big are they?

Question: Today's my day off. Do you think my 9th grade daughter would mind if I ate lunch with her in the cafeteria?
Answer: Shucks no. You could cut her meat and everything.

Question: Did you know your valedictorian cheated on her finals?
Answer: No, but I heard your kid did and he mustn't be very good at it.

Question: Why don't you have clear guidelines for choosing cheerleaders?
Answer: Next year we will. Only orphans will try out.

Question: What would you do if you lived near the school and your son's so-called friends threw trash in your yard every day?
Answer: Move.

Question: How many Division I college athletes does your athletic program produce?
Answer: Not many, but we've had hundreds of Division I parents.

Question: Where do teenagers learn such vulgar language?
Answer: At home.

Excuse Me! 'My science project exploded on the way to school.'

Great Ones Are Crackers

There are many good teachers and a few great ones. A look at the great ones can lead to weird conclusions regarding their (or the system's) sanity.

Chris captivates bored seniors, teaching them civics and economics. He's a part-time prune farmer who motivates students with letters from a mysterious Aunt Gussie in Tuscaloosa. Aunt Gussie's grey haired likeness, which has a strong resemblance to Chris, hangs on his wall. He calls his classes family and wears gaudy safari neckties on test days because his seniors need to know "It's a jungle out there!" Amazingly, they take both him and Aunt Gussie seriously. Chris was once 'Teacher of the Year.' He credited Aunt Gussie.

When I first met Tim, he was an off-the-wall, long-haired house painter with an unused teaching credential. At the time, he lived in a cave or a tree somewhere in the mountains near Manton. As a teacher, he gets kids to enthusiastically do things that border on the bizarre. His magic runs from teaching African drumming to yoga to levitating on top of Mt. Lassen. Most of all, he instills in kids the confidence to take risks and pursue their dreams. He was named 'Teacher of the Year for District 9.' When asked what it meant, he said he had no idea, but got a free meal, took the award and ran.

We hired Cleo even though she had been in three different schools in the previous four years. Maybe the moves had to do with the fact that Cleo is not good with details. She holds the record, with over 700 unanswered e-mail and voice mail messages. She also is the most dynamic and successful drama and English teacher any of us have ever seen. Reciting *Hamlet* from memory, she can get Red Bluff rednecks to lust for Shakespeare and most anything else she presents. When named county 'Teacher of the Year,' she attended the awards dinner under protest, since she had a rehearsal scheduled for that evening.

Fred is a chemistry teacher who takes the term 'mad scientist' to frightening levels. One of two 8th grade graduates of nearby Plum Valley School, Fred claims he was class valedictorian. Nonetheless, his college supervisor tried to counsel him out of the teaching program. Wearing worn cowboy boots and a different ball cap every day, his chemistry program is legendary. Kids fight to get into his classes and then learn to do things like scream "shove it " in unison when he asks them what to do with the decimal point. His classes are rigorous and few fail. He highlights each year with the Chemistry Affair. It is a black tie event in the gym with boys in tuxedos, girls in fancy gowns, apple cider fountains, a gourmet luncheon, live entertainment, three TV stations – all in the name of celebrating a year of chemistry. Fred has been nominated for numerous awards, but no one remembers - not even Fred - if he has actually received any.

These are great teachers; the ones kids say make a difference in their lives. Yet, a rational person could dismiss them as being a bit too crackers for such a noble and serious profession. There's a message here somewhere.

Excuse Me! 'Darrell spranged his foot.'

It's the Stupid People

Mrs. Piaga

Italian is such an expressive language. There are Italian words that are perfect descriptions and defy accurate translation. Even the way they are intoned and pronounced adds to their clarity and flavor. 'Piaga' is such a word. It was one of my father's favorites. If he called someone a piaga, you knew exactly the kind of person he was describing. Even if you knew no Italian, just the way he said it would give you a clear picture.

My English/Italian dictionary defines a piaga as a 'sore, scourge or whiner,' but that doesn't quite get it. My dad would have probably settled for 'pain in the ass,' but that also doesn't do it justice. You try to avoid piagas at all costs. Anyway, piaga is the only word I know that describes Mrs. Flowers.

It was bad enough that she was a piaga of the highest order, but why did her condition have to be compounded by a run of bad luck? When I couldn't slip out the back door of my office, I handled her whining about classroom temperatures and attendance errors. A nuisance, but that comes with the territory. Something stupid in a previous life must have made me deserve the following turn of events.

Her son was a rather normal kid, prone to do his own thing, but generally not a troublemaker. It seems he asked his math teacher if he could go to the bathroom. On his way to the bathroom, he got sidetracked and ended up in the gym, where some of his buddies were playing volleyball in their P.E. class. He joined them.

I have no idea why the teacher did not notice this one kid without his P.E. clothes on, but she didn't. She also missed his getting smacked in the nose with the ball and the blood flying all over the place. Leaving a trail of blood, he ran from the gym and into the counseling center to see the school nurse.

The nurse was not in, nor was her aide. I have no idea where they were or why none of the clerical staff or students noticed this kid with blood all over his clothes. He then went outside and called the piaga from the pay phone in front of the office. She hurried to school and found her son sitting on the front steps of the office, covered with blood with no one else around.

She rushed him to the hospital and they treated his broken nose which eventually required $2000 worth of rearranging. From the hospital, she called the school, only to discover that everyone thought he was in math. The math teacher had forgotten that he had left. She abruptly hung up.

Two days later, the boy returned to school, but had a mid morning doctor's appointment. Piaga came to pick him up and a student aide was sent to his classroom to get him, but returned saying the entire class was gone. Someone figured out that the class was on a field trip to City Hall and would return in twenty minutes. She asked to use the phone to tell the doctor they'd be late. The student at the desk told her that office phones were for business and to go outside and use the pay phone. She did. If there was still blood on it, she didn't mention it.

While waiting, she asked about his math book. It seems no one had picked it up in the room and it was lost. She was directed to the bookkeeper and told that she owed $34 for the missing book. During all of this, none of the regular staff (including me) ever saw her. I don't know where we were or what we were doing. My only excuse is that piagas just naturally trigger avoidance.

Now it is too painful to recreate the hours I listened to the piaga as a result of this fiasco. I was at her mercy. Especially, since I am always shooting my mouth off on how friendly and concerned we are. It had all happened; the blood trails were ample evidence. There was no defense for the events that happened. Profuse and sincere apologies have no effect on piagas. I just listened, and listened, and listened. I'm also sure it ain't over. Piagas have memories like elephants and they never go away.

"Sometimes I wonder if the world is being run by smart people who are putting us on or imbeciles who really mean it."

- Mark Twain

Excuse Me! 'I got locked in my bedroom.'

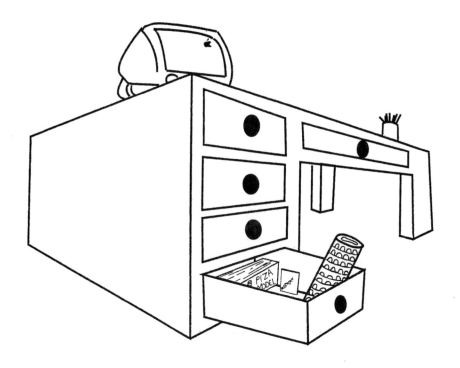

Bottom Drawer

Joe was cramming stuff in this drawer at an age when colleagues were seeking career or personal changes and advancements. During this time, he encountered some of these seekers and those experiences did little to foster his own ambitions. A few would say he had become cynical, while others expected him to move to Italy.

M.B.

Principals Care, Yes They Do

You've Got To Care

As a principal, there are times you don't know how much you care about your students and teachers. The trick is to not let anyone know how much you don't know you care. Two such incidents come to mind.

Amanda's letter was one of those feel good moments that come along every so often. A bright eyed and attractive girl, she's now on with her life and doing well in college. The other day she took time to write and thank her old principal. What a deal, made my day. It should be mentioned that Amanda was also a bit different. Strong willed and her own person, she had a few discreet tattoos and not so discreet pierced body parts - and I'm quite sure I hadn't seen them all.

Her letter noted that I'd "made a difference in her life." At a time when she "was in trouble and no one seemed to care, you took time to check how I was doing and support me," she wrote. She confessed that she still has a hard time believing that any principal would care enough to call a student in every week just to make sure she was doing okay. She apologized for not having told me sooner what a great guy I was and how lucky the kids at school were to have me. She promised to keep in touch.

So hard to be humble. What can you say after a letter like that? Well, what you don't say is the truth. Appearing mature, a good student, bright and articulate, Amanda was chosen for the Italian exchange program partly because of her uniqueness. I was the chaperone. Not long after being selected, she had the misfortune of being arrested for being drunk and disorderly in public. Her newly appointed probation officer called her a "nasty drunk with a foul mouth."

I'd heard enough. I called Amanda into my office, thinking there's no way I take this thing to Italy. If I'm going to be part of an international incident, it should at least be me who's drunk and disorderly. She was going to get the bad news straight out. I had not planned on her being charming, forthright and honest. Told me the whole story. Showed remorse, didn't blame others. Said she wouldn't take herself if she were the chaperone.

Weakening as I spoke, I told her we all make mistakes, blah, blah, blah. Not sure that I hadn't been conned, she left my office still on the exchange list. However, I promised myself no slick Lolita was going to bamboozle this veteran. I was going to pay attention, call her PO and personally check on this twit every week. If everything wasn't absolutely perfect, off she goes. So I called her in every week for the six weeks prior to the trip. I checked if her hands were steady, eyes were clear and her PO was happy. I also must have inadvertently said some encouraging sounding things.

Amanda did fine on the trip and was actually very adaptable, intellectually curious and one of our best ambassadors. I guess she never knew that my caring was more about covering my own tail than caring about her. Reminded me of the time, Mrs. Wooster, the volleyball coach, brought me a rose. It was another time my caring was above and beyond what one might expect from a principal.

It was a rainy, windy and cold day. My daughter, Michelle, came into my office after school, asking to use the car. I gave her the car keys. "We're just running to the ice cream shop, we'll be right back." The office closed, I was the only one left. Finished with what I was doing, I went outside to see if the car was in the parking lot. The office door locked behind me and without keys, I was stuck in the rain. I was getting drenched. I imagined Michelle and her friend, dry and warm, cruising around town with the stereo blaring. I was pissed and very cold.

Lights were on in the nearby gym and I could see kids and a teacher running around inside. I ran through the rain and into the gym. Cold and sulking, I leaned against the gym wall, keeping one eye on the parking lot. The custodian came by and I could see she wasn't thrilled with me tracking and dripping water and mud on her gym floor. Michelle finally pulled up and I ran out to the car, got in and crabbed at her for being late.

The next morning, first thing, our seasoned volleyball coach was waiting outside my office when I arrived. Mrs. Wooster was from the old school, a hard worker, one of those teachers who never, ever makes a social visit to the principal's office. This had to be important. With a tear in her eye, she presented me with the rose. "I've been coaching twenty years and not once has an administrator cared enough to visit a practice. I don't know how to thank you." I told her I was just doing my job and her practice looked terrific.

Both Amanda and Mrs. Wooster loved me for what I didn't even know I did. A lucky principal can sometimes care even when he doesn't. Faking it is the key.

"Sincerity is the key to this business. Once you can fake that, you've got it made."

- Monte Clark

Excuse Me! 'He watched a friend of the family die and was too upset to go to school.'

Aw Nesta Gawd This Really Happened

Levi

Levi may hold the school record in stupid stunts. Just trying to be funny and never intending to hurt anyone, Levi has been a master at creating mini-disasters that usually just irritate the hell out of most everybody. He always gets caught, tries lying and pays the price. By the skin of his teeth, Levi may graduate this year. The problem may be too many tardies and cuts in history for which he could lose a very necessary credit. Hey, but Levi had a plan.

Every bit as slick as Sean Connery, Levi slipped into the teacher's desk and found the attendance book. He didn't quite understand those lines and symbols used for attendance, but it couldn't be too hard to change those frequent tardy symbols that followed his name. Quickly and deftly, Levi extended those marks from partial lines to full lines.

As Levi's luck would have it, he changed the tardies to unexcused absences, an adjustment his graduation prospects didn't need. To make matters worse, three classmates witnessed his crime. Levi's style had never enhanced his popularity or the odds of the witnesses not snitching on him. They immediately squealed to the teacher and she sent the boy to me.

Levi's first line of defense had always been lying and he was pretty good at it. The threat of witnesses, evidence or fingerprints rarely knocked him off course. He could look you straight in the eye and deny most anything. Levi told me he had never, ever touched his teacher's book and, in fact, was a bit miffed that I would question his integrity.

For once, I could agree with the boy. The teacher and witnesses must have been in error. I told him we would go with whatever was in the book. Graduation may be a problem with so many absences, but he was going to leave with his honesty and integrity intact. Levi left my office a bit befuddled. He returned in about five minutes, wanting to reopen the discussion. I told him to put his proposal in writing and we would talk about it.

The next day he presented me with a written confession, with details, excuses and apologies for the crime. It included a suggestion to just forget the whole thing, since he had now seen the light. He insisted that he was lying before, but not this time. He had witnesses, he said. I tore up his confession and chastised him for returning to his lying ways.

Levi is not happy with me. He thinks I am lying to screw him out of a diploma. I assured him that principals only lie to liars. I told him if he has no more tardies, absences or lies, the two of us could sneak into her room and change her book. We'd be good partners in crime, since he knows where she keeps the book and I understand those symbols.

Excuse Me! 'My mother's too fat to walk to the Welfare Office, so I had to go for her.'

Aw Nesta Gawd This Really Happened

Wayne

Wayne, our performing arts director, came into my office today after school. That's normal, he comes in a lot. We had become good friends. He'd built our performing arts program into a thriving series of positive events that are great for our kids. I suspected he had one more wild hair of an idea for the program. He said he had some very interesting news for me. Sounded normal, he is a very creative teacher, always pushing the envelope. He said he'd be back teaching here in the fall. That was good news, he'd built a model program. He then said he'd be a woman. That was indeed *very* interesting news. I nearly wet my pants.

Calmly, Wayne asked me what I knew about transgenders. Not much, I admitted. Must have something to do with drag queens, I thought. Wasn't there a tennis player who did something like that once? He then explained that he'd been living a painful double life as a woman trapped in a man's body. He was going to do a sex change this summer. Maintaining his keen sense of humor, Wayne dryly acknowledged that this wasn't the typical summer institute for teachers that he was asking me to understand, support and I guess sort of approve.

The timing was right for him. His kids were grown, we have a good School Board and he suspected our thirteen year friendship would survive. It was time for him to be true to himself. For me, it sounded like the time for him to wear a dress. His wish and hope was to stay at our school while avoiding tar and feathers in our red neck haven. He gave me the name of another principal who had a teacher do this at his school. What did I think?

WHAT DID I THINK?? My God, I'd never even thought about this one - ever, not even a little bit.   We'd had gay teachers come out of the closet, but they looked the same as when they'd been in there. Wayne in a dress? He's real tall, heavy beard, slightly balding. I was trying to imagine what he'd look like. He told me he looks okay as a woman. Nonetheless, people were going to notice. No doubt about it.

He joked that I always pushed tolerance and diversity. This could be my big chance - push it to a new level. This would definitely be a new level. I suggested he do the *Black Like Me* thing and really go for it. Come back as a black woman.

I then learned a bunch of things that I didn't know and probably never hoped to know. No one chooses to be transsexual, it's a medical condition, there are more than we think, insurance doesn't cover operations, it's not a drag queen thing, there's a difference between feminine and effeminate, hormones are part of it and so on. He'd thought about and researched this a lot - as long as he could remember, in fact.

As usual, kids were his main concern. He'd leave the district if he needed to. Caring about and being sensitive to kids has always been his (her?) trademark. Yes, yes, that's a woman thing. Perhaps I should have known. How do we keep kids from being harmed by the inevitable storm around the him to her thing? I had no clue. There were no administrator workshops on this one. None that I'd been to. Trust me.

We talked quite a while longer. Everyone in the office had gone home. Just Wayne and I and my really, really dumb questions. What bathroom will you use? What will we call you? He kept encouraging the questions. Are knives involved in changing? Are there pills? We laughed a lot, made up some sick jokes, imagined and mimicked the reaction on certain faculty faces. Wayne pointed out that we were real lucky he's not an ag teacher or football coach.

This definitely would be a page in my book. Wayne felt if I couldn't get a chapter out of this one, it was going to be a crappy book. I was proud of myself. We may both get tarred and feathered, but I was curiously pleased that Wayne's inner hell would finally end. She is a very fine person. She'll be damn near seven feet tall in heels.

The next day I called that other principal. My first words were "We've never met, but definitely have something in common; I, too, have a transgender teacher." "Oh shit," he said, "let me close the door." We had a pleasant conversation, sharing similar reactions and experiences, and concluded that we were members of a rather small and unique club.

"The times they are a changin'"

- Bob Dylan

To Whom It May Concern:

As a parent of a short freshman, I am writing in regards to the recent casting of Oliver, where two of the lead roles were given to children not in high school. First of all, I thought the performing arts was for the benefit of high school students, not for younger kids. Is this fair to High Schoolers? I can somewhat see that the role of Oliver was meant for a small person, but there are many at your school. You probably even have midgets who deserve a chance. I would like to see something done about this.

> *Signed,*
> *A Concerned Parent*

Excuse Me! 'I had a test to find out who my biological father is.'

Aw Nesta Gawd This Really Happened

Principal of the Year

Most principals have plaques and things hanging on their office walls that show they've been honored for important stuff. I've never had many of those decorations, mainly because no one ever gave me any. I think you have to go to a lot of boring meetings and then keep your mouth shut when you do go in order to qualify for these awards. I did neither and that's my excuse. Others said I simply didn't deserve any.

Hey, but today I got the Principal of the Year Award for Tehama County. It was awarded at the annual administrators' kickoff breakfast at the golf club. I got up early, dusted off my wingtips and looked through my closet for a power tie. My lovely wife, whose job it is to keep me humble, stayed in bed. Having not been so awarded before, I wasn't sure I had the clothes that the others who get these awards wear. I'd missed most of the meetings where I could have scoped out what the winners wore.

So I asked my wife if I looked the part before I left. She verified that my clothes all sorta matched. She then asked how many schools there are in Tehama County. I told her about twenty-five. She then asked how many years I've been a principal in the county. Again, about twenty-five. It was her clever observation that they gave me the award this year because everyone else had gotten it and they needed to start over.

I headed out the door for the breakfast anyway, even though I knew there might have been a bit of ugly truth in what she said. After twenty-five years, I should have at least one of those of plaques on my wall. Besides, if what she said was true, it served them right to have to look me in the eye and give me a plaque.

As soon as everyone got their scrambled eggs and orange juice, the charter president introduced the winner, me. They expected me to say something, and again I hadn't attended enough meetings to know exactly what the Principal of the Year winner is supposed to say. So I thanked them and told them what my lovely wife had said before I left. There were a few nervous chuckles, which leads me to believe there may have been some truth to her quip. I think they thought I was a smart ass who wasn't appropriately grateful for the honor.

It was an okay experience, except that I didn't get a plaque. They gave me this glass apple. Really, a blue glass apple. It's a pretty apple, but how do you hang a glass apple on your office wall? It's from one of those fancy glass blowing places and very nice, but there's not even anything engraved on it. No card was with it saying I was Principal of the Year. I could have gotten the apple for being Fruit of the Year.

In fact, one of my loyal vice principals insists it's an award for Idiot of the Year. Maybe it is. Anyway, I gave it to my lovely wife, who deserves something for working so hard at her job of keeping me humble. She says I should cherish the glass apple, since I probably won't last until they get to me in another twenty-five years.

Excuse Me! 'I stayed at a friend's house and she was late, not me. I was just with her.'

To: Faculty

From: Joe

Re: Important News

One of our teachers will be discussing with students an upcoming gender transition. This is a recognized medical/psychological condition and is being done with full cognition of the Administration and School Board.

While you may hear about this in your classrooms, we must respect rights to privacy and not engage in classroom discussions. Specific questions should be directed to me.

Floods, bus wrecks, fired sups, deaths, drug busts, suicides, fires, vandalism. Special memos, just type them up, run them on bright paper and put them in the mailboxes. People read them and do what they need to do. However, this transgender issue was in a league of its own. A few staff members had already talked to Wayne and several had even seen his photos.   Most had no clue.

A few thought this memo was my sick sense of humor pushing things a bit over the edge. A few, after gasping, laughing or screeching and verifying who it was, sought out Wayne to offer their support. Some took the lighter path, getting together to each call our all-too-macho vice principal proclaiming their sensitivity. I do wish I had taken time to write down all the one-liners that this thing induced. Things like "Yippee, another cheerleading advisor candidate" or "Joe, you and Mike Wallace were made for each other" or "This gender equity crap is out of hand."

The afternoon of the memo, Wayne told his sixth period concert choir class that he was going to look real different in the fall. The school psychologist was there just in case. Just in case of what, we didn't know. His students asked some good questions. They were very supportive. Finally one asked, "Can we sing now?" The psychologist said when she left, they were singing *Danny Boy.* I guess most students hadn't had enough training in bigotry to be horrified. I'm not sure it was the same when they told their parents at the dinner table.

"A closed mind is a wonderful thing to lose."
- Mickey Bitsko

Excuse Me! 'I was in class. It's not my problem if no one saw me.'

Aw Nesta Gawd This Really Happened

Jennifer

After a while, principals just get shock proof. They've seen and heard it all in their offices. I am no longer blown away by the weird; I expect it. When the tall blonde woman walked in during summer school with our young music teacher, I didn't suspect a thing - for about thirty seconds. It took that long to recognize Wayne, er, Jennifer.

When I realized who he/she was, I said nothing. Absolutely nothing. I 'd thought about my first encounter a number of times. I had rehearsed some clever lines. When it arrived, I didn't remember them and didn't have an opening line. I ended up not saying much of anything. I wasn't rude, but there's really no etiquette for this type thing. Or at least any that I've ever heard about. "Nice to meet you" didn't sound right. "Congratulations" seemed a bit much. "What's new?" a bit flippant. "Nice outfit" just wouldn't come out of my mouth, since, fashion wise, she looked rather ordinary to me. There's no doubt in my mind that Miss Manners would have fumbled this one. I did say she looked like his daughter or his daughter looked like her or something like that.

I just talked to Jennifer as if she were Wayne. It was awkward, but not uncomfortable. I kept screwing up the pronouns. We talked about things, not girl things, just things. I liked Wayne. I'm sorta sad he's gone, but I think Jennifer will be okay.   I was so pleased that she wasn't a bimbo. Okay to be a woman, but I had a fear she'd be a bimbo. I guess I imagined that if Jennifer would go this far she wasn't going to settle on being a regular broad and maybe she'd flaunt all of the pre-feminist stereotypes with gobs of makeup, leather, spiked heels, flipping her hair and all.

To my relief, after the first thirty seconds, it wasn't a big deal. That fact itself is shocking when I think about it. A few zealous preachers were going bazooka in their churches, some parents were real nervous, the media was frothing and circling like piranhas, 20/20 was on the phone and everyone else was curious as hell. A friend and talented male teacher was now painting her nails, wearing a blonde wig, sporting a pretty dress and had changed God knows what else - and it's no big deal to me!

I am either lucky or oblivious. Not everyone was able to get through their first meeting as casually. Most folks did a serious double take and sputtered something. One of the secretaries giggled that "Her boobs are bigger than mine." Another nervously blurted, "I don't loan clothes." Our athletic director looked her in the eye and stammered, "Can you be the cheerleading adviser?"

In the end and after the initial shock, few people said or did much of anything. Several zealots came to Board meetings and threatened lawsuits, hell, fire and damnation, but they had done that before on other issues. A strange woman made a presentation that contained some serious anatomical errors. These folks were neither parents nor saints and so far "out there" that Jennifer seemed normal. Most everyone else just got on with things. I think weirdness has run its course. There's not much left that's not normal. Jennifer's concert choir sounds the same as Wayne's.

Excuse Me! 'The kitten knocked over the alarm clock. Honest!'

Mickey Who?

Bitsko

People ask me about Mickey Bitsko, a mysterious character intent on following the beat of his own drum. In spite of (or because of) his eccentric nature, he has been my friend and confidant. It bothers me that he gets called the darndest names. He's been called a hippie, a slacker, a weirdo and worse, all by people who never met him. It isn't fair. I am compelled to provide a defense, or at least a few excuses. Mickey would do the same for me.

Tim, a teacher and good friend, introduced me to Mickey. Tim's a bit strange in his own right, but Bitsko is even closer to the edge. He drifts in and out of our lives. Mickey is always entertaining and often the source of clarity and inspiration. He routinely sends Tim quotes that end up on a school bulletin board. They are things like "The best defense against logic is ignorance." Heavy stuff!

Mickey's quotes add spice to mundane and ordinary days. He also is quoted in reports to the state or other agencies when an important source appears necessary. He is then Dr. M. Bitsko. Not really unethical, since Mickey would say whatever we quoted if we asked him. Every time we've told him about a Dr. Bitsko quote, he's said, "Yes, I'da said that. Right on." What a guy!

Mickey is also a sports fanatic with a passion for our Holiday Classic tourney. Every year he submits to the *Daily News* and *Bluffer* off-the-wall articles and a page of Useless Sports Facts. The nature of his comments amuse a few and offend a few more.

Everyone deserves a friend like Mickey Bitsko!

Prep sports doesn't get any better

Daily News Holiday Classic Tourney shows off local youth

By MICKEY BITSKO
Mystery correspondent

Put aside the adventures of Monica, Bill and Saddam or whatever else graces the front page of this daily dispenser of truth and folly. Some things, like the youth of America, are really important. You've turned to the right page. It's basketball tourney time in Red Bluff, California, USA!!

Rumor has it that Bill Goodbody donated another old typewriter to the school, so it's once again the Daily News Holiday Classic - and what a classic it is. Sixteen talented high school teams from different states, different cultures, all descending on Red Bluff for four solid days of hoops. And there's the awesome rally, barbecues, cheerleaders, dancers, singers and a community that houses, feeds and loves the visitors.

High school athletics doesn't get much better than this, it's a great show. The participants will remember the Daily News Holiday Classic for the rest of their lives. So get off the couch and quit bellyaching about today's kids. Supporting these young men and women is more important than any drivel on the front page. You owe it to yourself to come and see first hand what's right with America's youth. These kids will play their hearts out, display great sportsmanship and the NBA can go suck an egg.

Mickey Bitsko is a "mystery correspondent" in that, while he often makes his views known in print, he has since the early 1960s remained hidden from the view of all but Red Bluff High Principal Joe "I Coulda Been a Baseball Pro" Peianconi. Little is known of Bitsko, other than he is *rumored* to be an omniscient, omnipresent sports fan, and *known* to be an unwavering supporter of youth and the philosophy that "ATTITUDE IS EVERYTHING!"

Excuse Me! 'She went to Reynolds Feed Supply to get some grass hay. Her steer has got the runs and won't make weight at the Fair.'

Rools and Roolers

Rules

Thomas Edison once said, **"There ain't no rules here. We're trying to get something accomplished**." I've got that quote hanging on my office wall. I'm sure Edison was probably talking about inventing light bulbs or something when he said it, but I think it's perfect for schools.

School people spend at least two-thirds of their professional lives thinking up rules and policies to solve problems, never understanding that rules can only deal with symptoms. A favorite is some schools banning bandanas, Raiders jackets, team caps and everything else that someone thinks is gang related. Boy, that rule will get rid of gangs. Good grief, with that rule you'd have *no* clue who the bad guys are.

A good indicator of my weirdness is my very own Raiders jacket. I bought it right after someone told me we needed a rule to ban them on our campus. I have always been a Raiders' fan, it's a warm jacket and it confused the hell out of the Hispanic kids who thought they were real cool wearing theirs. Snake Stabler would be proud.

Besides that, rules are very good when training animals, but is that how we want to get teenagers to be responsible adults? Subject them to simple pain/pleasure stimuli? But most discouraging is the fact, that in my experience, teenagers absolutely love to know the rule and take great delight in thinking of creative ways to subvert it. It's this subversion that keeps the smart ass grins on adolescent faces. There have been a lot of times when they've done it to me.

Corning is a nice town. Known as the 'Olive City,' they have a good high school and the Corning Cardinals are a very good football team. Prior to the big game, we don't need banners on our campus saying "Corning Sucks" or "Cards Are Tards."

I marched down to student council and in no uncertain terms told them that these banners were coming down and that we were having nothing that in any way derided a rival town, school or mascot. Those banners were offensive, in poor taste, the work of small minds, unacceptable, inflammatory, juvenile and so on.

I should have known I was being had when Anthony asked me to repeat the rule, so they could make sure they understood. I repeated that we would not allow deriding a town, school or mascot. He thanked me and said I had made the rule very clear. The banners came down immediately.

Thinking that principals just have to make clear rules sometimes, I felt pretty good until the next morning. I noticed immediately that we had brand new banners saying "We Hate Olives." Hey, what's the problem? Nothing derogatory about the town, school or mascot.

On another occasion, I chided student council for not using the $250 moving message board we bought for the cafeteria. We bought the thing so they could have interesting, school related messages and here it was the middle of November and the message board read "Happy Halloween." Can't the brightest kids in school do any better than that? The new rule is that you get something up there that keeps people informed, piques their interest, whatever.

The next day, the message board rolled the announcement **"Sign up for the student exchange with Shasta. See if their principal is as short as ours."** Hey, it's your rule. You said make it interesting.

My favorite example is Ryan, who had his driver's license for five whole days when he talked his parents into letting him take the family car to school. One of his parents' big rules was that no one rides in the car without a seatbelt on. Ryan's problem was that he had six friends wanting to go to lunch and only five other seat belts.

Let's think about this rule. No problem, really, we'll just put Mitch in the trunk. There's no parent rule or law against riding in the trunk without a seatbelt. This would have all worked out well if Ryan had not had the misfortune of getting into a Main Street fender bender with Mitch still in the trunk.

And he still may have been all right if the cop hadn't gotten there so quickly and Mitch hadn't started banging on the trunk lid. This piqued the policeman's curiosity and got Mitch out of the trunk. Ryan was right; there's no law against not wearing seatbelts in the trunk. I suppose his parents modified their rule. Hey, you said no one in the car without seat belts. What's the problem?

So, I look at Edison's quote every time I get the urge to make another rule. Why not get something accomplished?

"Rules are for those who fear making decisions."

- Mickey Bitsko

Excuse Me! 'My parents went on a cruise. Would you go to school if your parents were on a cruise?'

Aw Nesta Gawd This Really Happened

My B.S. Legacy

We have two daughters. We are proud of them. They are products of our maligned school system and have done well anyway (as have most everyone else's kids, by the way). One is an English teacher who just signed her first teaching contract.

There's something special about your own kid going into your chosen profession. It's like she's taking over the family business. You feel compelled to give some advice, talk about the thrills, warn about the alligators or maybe pass on a secret weapon. Figuring out what to do was not an easy task, but I did it.

Alisa is going to do well. She is well prepared, has great instincts, loves teenagers and possesses a keen sense of humor - and I'm not one bit biased. Nonetheless, like all young teachers, she'll need some help. It's so sad to see the good ones leaving to sell insurance and make money. So I thought about books she should read and classroom management tips. She can get any of that from her new principal or figure it out herself. It's the BULLSHIT stamp that will save her.

As a first year teacher, someone gave me this rubber stamp, a big one, that says BULLSHIT in big capital letters. Just pound that sucker in an ink pad and you can whomp it on any written or printed message. It instantly neutralizes whatever annoying communication a parent, colleague, administrator, county office, department of ed or governor chooses to send you. Without the stamp, one is relegated to opening mail, reading the nonsense, feeling awful and setting it aside just to have it taunt you again. This is devastating to someone who is excited, positive and oblivious to the lurking grumps and bureaucrats. With the stamp, you just whack it, put it in a special pile, then smile every time you look at it. It's therapy that gives you perspective and clarity.

So I passed on my BULLSHIT stamp to Alisa, with specific instructions. I told her to use it wisely and frequently, but wait till you have tenure before you stamp stuff and write 'return to sender' on it. Maybe I'll get her a RETURN TO SENDER stamp a few years down the road.

I'm quite pleased with what I've passed on. Alisa is going to make it and I'm proud as hell to have helped. I've never heard of a teacher leaving because of the kids. It's all the other crap that drives them crazy and into stock options and sales. Besides, I'm at a point in my career where I don't need the stamp. Principals get so much, I'd need a BULLSHIT stamping machine. I just say it straight out to anyone who's listening. I call them if I need to return it to sender.

My only fear is that technology will render the stamp obsolete. How do you stamp a computer screen? When everything starts arriving electronically, Alisa will have to find another means of categorizing and neutralizing the bullshit. Putting a BULLSHIT sticker on the 'delete' button is a thought. She's a bright kid. She'll figure something out and at least one school will be better off for it. I'm so proud.

Excuse Me! 'When I woke up this morning my Dad had died during the night. I'll try to be in this afternoon.'

Aw Nesta Gawd This Really Happened

Maul at Mill Creek

Superintendents have an even shorter shelf life than principals. They tend to come and go, but I've gotten along with a number of them. I didn't even buy one of the buttons at a National Association of Secondary School Principals' convention that read '*Happiness is Your Superintendent's Picture on a Milk Carton.*'

One, however, provided for some new experiences. They called it a Board Retreat at Mill Creek Resort. It was really a Saturday Board meeting with the ten administrators. Mill Creek Resort is so far away from anywhere that it was a poorly disguised secret meeting to hash out the "problems" that arose with the hiring of a new superintendent.

The new superintendent is a nice enough guy. The resume he showed us on opening day proved that he'd done some important things. He and I get along well enough. However, when he talks about school stuff, it reminds me of the first time I went to Germany. I think I know what I should be hearing, but I can't understand a single word of it. That's not entirely his fault. I never learned German either.

To his credit, he knows many laws, rules, codes and policies that I should at least have heard about. His top down, law and order approach has worked for him, but is quite contrary to the creative chaos that we promote and our staff has learned to love. Suffice to say, neither of us has been enamored with the other's style. The staff is confused, concerned and cantankerous. Consequently, it appears the Board has either made a mistake in hiring him or another, in not firing me and a few others.

Staff was getting very wary and skeptical of my constant assurances that "It'll be all right." So was I. Television spots, newspaper articles and packed Board meetings have been verifying the lack of harmony. So off to Mill Creek we went.

This Board is a very good one. They range from a bright, articulate surgeon, who admittedly delegates nothing ("except maybe some things to the girls in the office") to a reformed hippie, who's now a very successful park ranger. The other three are somewhere in between. All are good people, wanting to do the right thing.

The meeting opened with the Board president asking the supe to sit off to the side and say nothing. I was then the recipient of some very pointed questions. They were queries like "Are the teachers loyal to you because you never fire any of them?" I said "Huh?" and "I don't understand the question" several times. It was tense, or as the doctor later noted, "There was a perceptible increase in the group's sphincter tone index." The other administrators baled me out with some catchy buzzwords like 'collaboration' and 'empowerment.'

What followed were several hours of philosophy-type talk that seemed to bring us together. This was good. The word 'student' was used a lot. People were understanding what they had and what they hired. It was clear the new boss had been given a tough assignment. It would have been tough for almost anyone to jump in and lead this unique creation. There was even some general consensus on what they wanted the system to look like from here on out.

However, there remained one slight problem. The new boss was still off to the side, where he'd been exiled and muzzled. I am sure I was the not the only one to notice that we'd experienced a seance, minus one, but as usual, I was the first to open my big mouth. We had talked a lot about inclusion, but the boss was not included.

I mentioned that we had an upcoming staff meeting Tuesday morning. Staff was not quite to a lynch mob mentality, but it would be important that we have something semi-profound to say at the meeting. The staff needed some good reason to put away the picket signs. A memo stating "We are continuing our efforts to ameliorate our differences in a manner that is beneficial to all concerned" was not going to cut it.

Tension was again in the air. Awkwardly, everyone looked at the exiled boss. Again, I opened my mouth with, "Do you want to be part of our culture?" "Yes," he said. "Even if it gets you out of your comfort zone?" I probed. "Like I'm not out of my comfort zone now? Of course, I can do whatever it takes," he retorted.

"All right, here's my idea. . . Tuesday morning. . . the staff meeting in the library opens with the usual announcements. A siren is heard outside. You and I are carried in, all bloodied up, on stretchers, by the other administrators. You jump off the stretcher, stagger to the podium, give one line about 'we worked it out, we're a team. I want to be one of you.' I'll guarantee it will work. Staff will see you as a human, caring person, able to work with them on their level. Can you do it?"

His answer was a quick, "Yes!" A board member then insisted that he wanted part of the 'Gorilla Theater' and to help with a stretcher. He wanted some blood on him, also. The doctor offered to be part of the "psychodrama" and "come in Monday, all bloody." "Great, but make it Tuesday, with the rest of us." One wanted a stethoscope to announce to staff that he does have a heart. Another expressed relief that they weren't asked to be pall bearers. We then broke for lunch.

It was unbelievable to me that these normal looking people had so gleefully jumped into a world of absurdity and borderline insanity. Absolutely amazing to me what folks will do to reduce the sphincter tone index. Definitely the strangest Board meeting I'd ever been to. Stay tuned . . .

"What people have said about me, both good and bad, are about the same."

- Willie Nelson

Excuse Me! 'Excuse Holly from school yesterday as she stayed home to take a laxative. She will be staying home every Wednesday from now on as she has a chronic constipation problem and needs to take a laxative on Wednesday.'

Tuesday . . . A Very Different Faculty Meeting

I've instigated some weird things, but this was definitely out of the ordinary, even for me. One teacher called it a "Zen moment." Another said it was "totally bizarro." One told me it was the "classiest thing you've ever done" (which probably says a lot about my 'class' ranking).

The participants planned to meet in the cafeteria at 7 A.M. I wore my tattered tennies, faded Everlast trunks, old 'Italian Stallion' bathrobe and not much else. I was there at 7 sharp and eager to do anything to get us out of the funk. The superintendent was the last to arrive, making the rest of us wonder if maybe he wasn't going to give us the ultimate snub. He had on some nice Nikes, UC Berkeley shorts and a new Hard Rock Cafe sweatshirt. The Board president wore a referee's shirt and the other Board members wore hospital green gowns. One of the administrators was in charge of makeup. We got black eyes and fake blood. All the props were in place. VP Bob gave us the scripts he'd written.

The staff had gathered in the nearby library for a 7:30 meeting and Jan was detailing some info about Back-to-School-Nite. They were tensely anticipating some info about the Saturday meeting. As planned, a police car pulled up behind the library and leaned on its siren. The Board members then ran in carrying me lying on a stretcher. They dropped me in front of the group and ran back out the door. They quickly returned with the superintendent and plopped him next to me.

There were nervous chuckles from the stunned group. A Board member in his ranger uniform traipsed in and announced, "The Maul at Mill Creek is over. The differences have been resolved." Another Board member ran over to me with her stethoscope, listened to my heart and said she thought I'd pull through. She then went to the boss, listened through the stethoscope and proclaimed, "He does have a heart!"

I then got to my feet, looked at my script card and said "I quit! - oh, this must be his card." That wasn't what my script said, but it seemed appropriate at the time and got a laugh. I then read the card. "The battle is over. Time to clear the battlefield and get on with taking care of our kids." The superintendent, who apparently had memorized his part, then said "Sorry about the nose, Joe." That got a hearty laugh. He continued with something about cooperating and getting on with business. The Board president, who, (with blacked out teeth, lots of blood and using a walker), seemed way out of character, said a few things to the group.

We then headed for the door, the superintendent and I with clenched fists, raised arms. The staff jumped to their feet, burst into a thunderous standing ovation. It had taken about five minutes. Staff headed for work, a bit dismayed, but in a very good mood. The makeup did not come off easily. Definitely the strangest faculty meeting I'd ever been to.

Excuse Me! 'My pet snake got out of its cage and I had to help Mom look for it.'

To: Faculty and Staff

From: Joe

Re: Change and Stress

As a school, we are entering a time of rapid, exciting and stressful change. Perhaps these items can assist us as individuals.

How To Handle Stress

- Jam tiny marshmallows up your nose and try to sneeze them out

- Use your Mastercard to pay your Visa bill

- Pop some popcorn without putting on the lid

- When someone says 'Have a Nice Day!' tell them you have other plans

- During your next meeting, sneeze and then loudly suck the phlegm back down your throat

- Find out what a frog in a blender really looks like

- Dance naked in front of your pets

- Put your toddler's clothes on backwards and send him off to preschool as if nothing were wrong

- Thumb through *National Geographic* and draw underwear on the natives

- Go shopping - buy everything - sweat in them - return them the next day

- Drive to work in reverse

- Read the dictionary backwards and look for subliminal messages

- Start a nasty rumor and see if you recognize it when it gets back to you

- Bill your doctor for the time you spent in his waiting room

- Get a box of condoms - wait in line at the check-out counter and ask the cashier where the fitting rooms are

Mickey Bitsko

Principal Thoughts *Bluffer*

Pants

It is probably safe to assume that there is not a single school in this country where the boys do not wear pants. In some private schools, they all wear the same kind of pants. That idea sounds rather boring, but it certainly mutes whatever fashion or other statements that some believe pants may make.

My current candidate for the most noticeable, if not outrageous, are those giant pants. You know the ones, where it appears that at least one more teenager could fit in them. They sort of look like solid colored clown pants that the clown holds up with red suspenders. These, however, do not look quite so secure, although I've never seen a pair fall down.

It is not clear to me what group here has adopted these baggy expressions of style. Maybe its ones who think they are skaters, since I sometimes see them carrying skateboards. They could probably fit a couple of boards inside as well. Makes sense to me.

Some say gangsters wear baggy pants. Maybe they do. In some schools, baggy pants are outlawed, since they can conceal weapons or are symbols of gang affiliation. This all gets rather confusing, since weapons also fit in backpacks and there are dozens of gang symbols. The pants aren't the problem, but rather the outlaws that are inside them. Why not outlaw the outlaws, regardless of what pants they wear?

Oh, but I digress. Anyway, like I mentioned, some of our students wear baggy ones. We know our students and gangsters they aren't. Besides, real gangsters break laws and stuff and no one is going to be able to flee the scene wearing those things.

Then there's the other extreme. It's those extra tight fitting Wranglers, which sometimes have that three inch faded circle on one rear pocket. They are usually so tight I don't know how they get anything in the pocket, let alone a can of stuff to rot their gums and create the circle. They must buy them that way, sort of like the little red tag on Levi 501's.

Which brings me way back to the pants I wore to school a hundred or so years ago. We wore those 501's and 'pegged' the legs so they'd fit real tight. However, that wasn't the disgusting part. We also insisted that our mothers not wash them. They had to have that shiny look. It was real cool that way, you know.

I also remember my Dad telling us we were real idiots for pegging our pants. "Just screwing up good pants," he'd mutter. It should also be noted that he often talked of the white cords he and his buddies wore during the Roaring 20's. And they didn't wash those either. Dirty white cords?! I had never heard of anything so stupid.

So, is there something we can learn from the pants we wear? Perhaps there is. Unless someone is using their trousers like a swatstika to intimidate others, it probably doesn't matter. It's just a matter of time until real baggy Wranglers worn down around the knees will be the rage.

Trying to classify people into good and bad guys based on the pants they wear may be a monumental waste of time. Several months ago, a guy wearing Wranglers broke into my house. I made no judgements. Jerks come in all sorts of pants - even 50l's.

Excuse Me! 'I was shoveling manure at the Bull Sale.'

It Ain't Me, Babe

Poo-Poo Happens

My wife sometimes wears a sweatshirt to her preschool that reads 'Poo-Poo Happens.' At preschool, that's probably true. Most anywhere else, there is someone or something to blame for everything that happens, even poo-poo. Not only blame, but it's almost one's duty to sue the hell out of them.

Our high school has been sued dozens of times and our insurance has paid out millions. Now school staff is not immune to dumb negligence, but most of these suits were from things that just happened, like poo-poo at the preschool. Many were accidents, where a kid was doing something stupid and, in several cases, even been warned by staff.

Others were just bad luck. Suzy slipped and broke an ankle; Johnny tripped and cut his finger in the table saw. These things just didn't happen. They sue, they win and there's no luck involved. There's no logic. For the school, it's just shut up, take the blame and pay up.

A neighboring school got sued, and lost, to a kid who fell through a sky-light. Seems he was up on the roof trying to break into the school. He was injured badly and got a huge settlement. He probably didn't even get cited for breaking and entering. Strange, you say. Not at all.

Just today, Sophie was messing around with a friend at break. A teacher was ten feet away, told them to cool it, but Sophie fell and konked her melon on the concrete. It took 15 stitches. Before the blood had coagulated, her mother was in our office saying we'd be sued. Was she blaming Sophie or bad luck? None of the above and she'll get something. Bet on it.

It must be that deep pockets thing. Schools have lots of insurance, so sue. Why not, it works. Everybody does it. Most of the suits are for an amount right below the liability value of the policy. What if schools didn't carry insurance? What would the jurors, who are also taxpayers, do if schools had to start hocking school busses and books to pay off dumb lawsuits? Just a thought.

It is also a lawyer employment service. Our neighbor's kid broke her arm while ignoring signs and riding a bike through school corridors on a Sunday afternoon. Two lawyers contacted her about suing. They must lurk in the lobbies of Emergency Rooms to learn these things. When we had an athlete die, the family was deluged with lawyer 'offers.' They'd all work on a percentage. It was like the big time college athlete who has to select an agent. They got a good one.

My favorite lawsuit, however, is the only one I remember that we did not lose. The judge actually ruled in our favor. It was special. I had resigned myself to having to sue someone to ever be on the winning side. The victory had to do with two 14 year olds making Molotov cocktails, tossing them and setting a large building on fire.

The arsonists admitted their crimes to Bargh, our VP, and me. They told us in great detail how to make a Molotov cocktail and what they looked like when they exploded on the side of the building. The next day, the police were involved. The detectives came to interview the suspects. Bargh tried to call the parents with no luck, so he and I took turns sitting in during the tape recorded interviews. We were very busy and not enjoying our roles as 'parents in absentia,' or whatever they call it.

The little meatballs made a slick transition from arsonists to liars. With the detectives, they would not admit to anything, probably on the advice of their 'poo-poo doesn't happen' parents. It was wasting a lot of our time. Finally, after several hours of changing their stories a lot and a little encouragement from Bargh and I, they fessed up. They went to court and were sentenced.

Bargh, I and the school then got sued for $900,000.00 for denying the little cherubs their civil rights. It seems we were accused of coercing them into telling the truth. In legal terms we, "imprisoned the plaintiffs, failed to notify the plaintiff's parents and compelled the plaintiffs to give incriminating statements."

The judge ruled in our favor and they got nothing. We could not believe the ruling. There were high-fives all over our office. It was one lone flicker of sanity in an endless barrage of legal poo-poo.

Even more exhilarating was a short statement in the judge's ruling. He wrote that "defendant Johnson (Bargh) was not to be commended for saying 'cut the bullshit.'" to the boys. He went on to explain, however, that "the statement was not such that would cause emotional trauma or violate any civil right." Wow!

Dammit, if only I could have been the one "not to be commended." To this day, I remain extremely jealous of Bargh. I'm sure he has that darned decree framed in his den. It proves that once in a long, long while, poo-poo really can happen.

"The day you take complete responsibility for yourself, the day you stop making any excuses, that's the day you start to the top."

- O. J. Simpson (Who?)

Excuse Me! 'I kept David home today because he's got the runs. He can't talk to you right now because he ran to the store.'

Aw Nesta Gawd This Really Happened

My New Job

Let me tell you about my new job. The school board fired the new superintendent. We hardly knew him, which may be just as well. Anyway, in one of those behind closed door affairs, they agreed to pay him for six months after he's long gone. That translates into "We ain't hiring a replacement for awhile." So they asked the rest of us to figure out how to muddle through. The plan is to make me an Assistant Supe, move the current Assistant up, etc. It means I'm still principal most of the time and then at the District Office some of the time. This is a short-term solution, they say, but I've heard that one before. That's how I got this principal job fourteen years ago.

The D.O. has never been a place I chose to hang around. I always felt people there were secretly hoping I wouldn't do or say something embarrassing. The thought of working there made me quiver. They probably felt the same. My professional experience at the D.O. had been limited to boring meetings or, with hat in hand, begging forgiveness.

Today was my first day there. The people are polite, charming and wonderful. They talk softly and smile when you look at them. You get the impression that they know what they are doing. The place is decorated tastefully, with oak and mauve type wallpaper and stuff. The staff room has real tile and the coffee smells good and real different. The reception room has attractive portraits of the board members on the wall. The school paper is neatly stacked on an oak coffee table. It is quiet in the D.O. Very, very quiet. When the phone rings, it makes this low, soothing sound. There is no background music. It reminds me of places that always make me nervous. It is like my taxman's office, except that he has elevator music. Anyway, I'm okay with the taxman because I don't expect to feel comfortable there and know I don't have to stay long.

I got right to work, went through the mail, wrote 'principal' on most of it. Isn't that what they do? I can throw it away in my other office. The secretary made me an appointment with a guy pissed off at the principal and wanting to talk to a 'higher up.' I drank some of that good smelling coffee. After my time at the D.O., I trudged back to my old job. It was the end of a normal day. When I walked into the main office, I talked to a harried mother at the counter who wanted to know if the JV basketball team had left for their tournament. Her daughter had forgotten her sports bra. The phone was ringing. I then saw a very sad, bloody-nosed kid sitting in a chair, waiting for his parents. He'd been suspended for fighting. Jean, everybody's favorite secretary, was loudly cackling about something she'd overheard. Melissa was waiting for me to write her a letter of reference for a scholarship application that was due tomorrow. There was an all-call saying that busses were leaving early today. I had five phone messages. I had to go. The boys' team played at 7 in Healdsburg.

I was home again. I'm not going to like the District Office stuff. My wife says I'm being a baby. "Give it time," she says in a soothing voice.

Excuse Me! 'It was bad communication. I thought I was suspended.'

November 16, 1987

Dear Sir/Madam Principal:

I'm 43 years old but can still recall the memories of distress, loneliness and resentment at always being on the tail end of the alphabetical order.

I always hated those long alphabetical lines and considered them to be unfare to those who were stuck in the back.

To me the alphabetical order can be compared to a caste system.

I felt a need to express myself about this to someone who could change it.

Take care.

Sincerely,

J. D. Wilson

Aw Nesta Gawd This Really Happened

The Gong Show

Faculty meetings can be oh so deadly. Usually it's a time where the administration rags on the teachers about something. A boring memo would suffice, but they won't read a boring memo. I never understood why anyone ever thought they'd listen to boredom with any more gusto than they'd read it. I always thought it was kind of like the futility of teaching a pig to sing – wastes your time and pisses off the pig.

Besides that, I have embarrassing recollections of what a jerk I was as a teacher during typical faculty meetings. And when an administrator can't induce narcolepsy, there are always a core of teachers who absolutely love to hear themselves talk. They stand up and everybody rolls their eyes in unison. So, as a principal, faculty meetings are certainly nothing I do simply because someone says you have them. I always carefully measure what my level of interest would be when writing an agenda. Consequently, we don't meet as a group very often.

Now sometimes there are actual dictates or other things that need to be shared with the entire group, but let's try to keep 'toxic waste disposal' and 'restroom supervision' as painless as possible. Do you know how long a teacher can expound on the differences between a tardy and an absence? With this in mind, I came up with the Gong Show idea for a morning faculty meeting.

I got one of those five minute egg timers and borrowed the big metal gong from the music teacher. We had about ten agenda items. Ten different staff members got five minutes each to make their presentation. I stood behind them and off to the side with the egg timer set beside me and the thing you whack the gong with in my hand.

The meeting was going great. The presenters were animated and talking fast, looking over their shoulders to make sure they weren't going to get gonged. The faculty was craning their necks to watch the egg timer and they were amused and awake, if not interested. People were smiling and laughing, the presenters running back to their seats beating the last grain of sand.

It was all great fun until the school psychologist got up there. She was sure her topic was a bit more important than the others. Therefore she talked at a normal pace and wasn't about to acknowledge the idiot principal and his goofy gong behind her. There was a murmur through the group as the final grains dropped. The was an awkward silence except for her chatter when I hit that sucker so hard it damn near knocked the windows out of the library. She was last on the agenda, so laughing loudly, the teachers all got up and headed for class.

She spent most of that day in her office, terribly upset with me. Our relationship was never the same after that. I think the psychologist thought I was crazy. She might have been right.

Excuse Me! 'Please excuse Sheila from PE due to craps.'

146

The Naked Truth According to Michael

Mr. Hassy,

Friday when you said that we could all go to your room a dirty picture got downloaded onto your computer. I don't know how it got downloaded but it was certainly not meant to happen.

When we went to your room, Shelby V. was on the computer like always and looking at different pictorials of celeberties. Later on he went to a pictorial of Cindy Crawford and it was clean and everything. Then I saw a menu so I just clicked on one of them and slowly started to appear was a blond looking girl and Shelby started to tell me to hurry up and click out of there so I somehow clicked out of there and that was that.

Then today I was called in to the office about something and I didn't have a clue what for. I was told somebody had downloaded a naked picture of some girl yesterday. I guess somehow a nude pictorial got downloaded onto your computer and I don't know how. I believe I downloaded it on accident somehow.

I don't even have the slightest clue how computers work and to download stuff. I'm really sorry I downloaded that stuff but I totally didn't mean any harm. I totally apologize for my actions. I'll never touch your computer again. Sorry.

— Michael

Aw Nesta Gawd This Really Happened

A Close Call

I can't deny it. I once applied for a superintendent's position. I really did. Never mind that I had laughed with other principals at those "Happiness is your supe's picture on a milk carton" cartoons at NASSP conventions. I even got an interview. I was a finalist, by gum. Hey, but don't jump to any conclusions. I can explain.

It was in my home town, my alma mater. I grew up in Geyserville, in the Sonoma County wine country, back when wine wasn't one bit chic. We were winos and dagos, but it was beautiful in the wine country, even then. There's lots of new money in the valley now and the small, unified school district has a great reputation. Our families still live there. An old friend from high school said "Joe, we've got good schools here and these yuppies are okay, but we need an asshole like you running things, know what I mean?" I sent in the papers I'd put together right after the 'Maul at Mill Creek.'

As one would expect, they had a bunch of applicants, who probably had doctorates, heavy resumes and nice clothes they wore even when they weren't interviewing. I was surprised when the headhunters called me for an interview. I didn't think whoever read the aps would have been impressed that I was a member of the Mickey Bitsko Heritage Association or that one of my professional accomplishments was having been a former student body president of their school. It had to have been the great letters I had, since I knew a lot of folks who owed me an exaggeration or two.

This was very different from the story my dad told about hiring a supe for the same district back when he was on the Board in nineteen fifty something. The county office selected three candidates and the Board met them at Catelli's, the local restaurant/tavern type place. The first guy was a no show. The second guy wouldn't have a drink with them. This was the wine country, so they hired the third applicant, who had quite a few drinks with them. As my dad said, "Who the hell would hire a guy who wouldn't even have a drink?" Their man stayed a long time and as my dad often said, "He ran a tight ship; he was a mean son-of-a-bitch when he was drinking and he was drinking a little bit all the time."

Although this s.o.b. was probably what my old friend had in mind when he encouraged me to apply, the process has changed a bit. Knowing that, I bought a new shirt, shined my wingtips and tried to remember what a power tie looks like. My wife and I spent the night before the interview with my mother. I got up early and headed the mile or so to the school for the 8 AM interview. When I walked into the office the secretary screeched, "It's little Joey!" Her family had lived across the street from us back before they'd probably even invented Chardonnay. She showed me into the superintendent's office, a very nice looking place with a big window looking out on row after row of my cousin's Cabernet and Chardonnay.

I was daydreaming about suckering grape vines right across the road. My cousin Rich and I still argue about who threw the dirt clod that hit Boney in the back of the head in that vineyard one afternoon. Carlos was there, but he was a nice guy and I'm pretty sure he didn't do it. I swear it wasn't me, but someone sure konked him. I'm not sure

Boney was ever the same. Anyway, the headhunter, a former sup in cowboy boots and ponytail, came in and gave me a writing assignment. I had fifteen minutes to write a retirement speech for a lousy employee. It was easy; I've done a few of those speeches, but I really wanted to write about my cousin, who hasn't told the truth about that dirt clod for nearly forty years.

The other headhunter (they work in pairs) was a very pleasant woman, who later took me into the first interview with what was called the Advisory Group. There were a lot of them and they all had a question. I told them there were more of them than were in my graduating class back when I went to this school. One of them was a cousin of mine who I'd only seen at a few funerals in twenty-five years and several others had familiar names. There were also some teachers, classified folks and some token minorities. They were very polite, but they didn't have a particularly happy aura about them. It went okay, I guess. I told them exactly what I thought, which probably wasn't the best job-getting strategy. Hey, but what the heck, trying to con them wasn't going to fly, since there were a few who remembered "little Joey" and weren't going to buy an act that was slicker than I was back when I wasn't very slick at all.

I then went into the second interview with the Board of Trustees. They were five of the nicest, brightest, most sincere sounding, articulate and sophisticated yuppies I'd been around in recent memory. My dad would not have gotten elected to this Board and there were definitely none of my high school pals or relatives in this group. They asked good questions and I answered every damn one. I didn't stutter even once. They were very difficult people for me to read. Where I'd been for a bunch of years, there was rarely any doubt where people were coming from - especially after I opened my mouth. I really didn't know if these folks liked me or thought I was a complete idiot.

Apparently, I did all right, or at least a majority felt sorry for the old alum, since the next day they called to tell me I was a finalist. The Board wanted me back for another interview. They wanted to talk about budgets and assessment and some other stuff that isn't at the top of my fun list. We'd also had time to check out the prices of real estate in the wine country. The only good housing news was that my mother has a big house. In talking with the locals, it seems there were also a few little snags at the old alma mater. That Advisory Group was divided into at least three rather grumpy camps; old timers, teachers who had their own candidate and sassy Latinos. None were very happy campers. The Board was looking for a "strong leader" to pull things together, another way of saying there was going to be some ass kicking to do.

I'd been there and done that and it didn't make for fun times. Some of the kickees would probably have been old pals and relatives. Sounded to me like they needed a yuppie who's drinking a little bit all the time. They were not going to buy my shared decision making, collaborative, win/win b.s. I could have faked the yuppie and done the drinking, but slash and burn management was for someone else. So I called the headhunters. It was thanks, but no thanks. It was a close call, but it's back to cafeteria duty, judging science projects, complaining parents, hogs at the fair, water balloons and homecoming queens. And that's just the first two weeks of school.

Excuse Me! 'I had a job interview for a job I didn't really want.'

149

Stupidest Questions Ever Asked By the Media and the Answers
I Didn't Give

Question: The last time I had you on the air was in the Oakland Coliseum and your girls were playing for the state basketball championship. You talked about how great school spirit was. Well, you've now lost 5 straight football games and are down 21 - 0 at halftime. Has school spirit dropped at all?
Answer: Oh hell no. The kids are real excited about getting thrashed every week. We're on a roll - the coaches tell me we can lose 'em all.

Question: Last night's fire loss is estimated at $2 million. What are your plans on rebuilding?
Answer: My palm reader and I predicted this fire years ago. We have detailed rebuilding plans. Unfortunately, I think they burned up in the fire.

Question: Your senior test scores dropped this year. What caused the decline?
Answer: This is the stupidest senior class I've ever seen. They are all going to have to get jobs with newspapers.

Question: Do you have any comment on the letter to the editor's accusation that the administration misappropriated funds?
Answer: Do I ever, but I think I'll withhold comment because I understand hallucinations often accompany severe nymphomania and that she is trying to get help.

Question: The bond election lost by a two to one margin. Any plans for another election?
Answer: Do the words 'Little Big Horn' mean anything to you?

Question: What precipitated the disciplinary action of your quarterback?
Answer: He punched a nosy journalist.

"Be good and you'll be happy, but you won't get your name in the news."
- Mickey Bitsko

Excuse Me! 'My parents made me visit a college I have no chance of ever getting into.'

Aw Nesta Gawd This Really Happened

Kristy

It was a note from a regular tipster that led me to search Kristy's purse. One might question whether the word of a chronic snitch was probable cause, but Kristy looked as much like she might carry a few narcotics as a cheerleader looks like she might carry lip gloss. She had interesting body piercings, amateur tattoos, greasy hair and that 'hunted' look in her steely cold eyes.

The purse turned out to be a real jackpot - a lot of drug paraphernalia, a baggie of marijuana, some pills and two mean-looking, switchblade-type knives. The charges included possession of marijuana and concealed weapons. This warranted felony charges, suspension, expulsion; definitely serious stuff. The police hauled her away.

The next morning Kristy was out of juvenile hall and back in my office with her mother. Mom was relatively young in years, but, like her daughter, looked like her odometer had been around a time or two. She was actually kind of scary looking. She apologized for leaving her lower teeth at home, plopped Kristy's books on my desk and literally spit out the following: "I'm withdrawing Kristy from this school. She won't get a fair deal here. Those knives I gave her so she could protect herself from Mexicans. The dope wasn't hers; she just had it to protect a friend. I'm taking her right now to enroll her in the continuation school. They'll treat her fair." I replied, "That may not be possible. You see, the continuation school is in the same district and she may be expelled from the district. Mr. Garcia, the Mexican principal over there, probably won't enroll her."

"Well, she ain't going here. You won't give a kid a break." I asked why they'd let her out of the hall and she said that it was too full of real criminals. They left. I looked through the books she'd left on my desk. There were some disgusting notes. I next saw Mom and Kristy in court. As is usually the case, I felt like I was the one on trial. I got a lot of questions on the stand about how and why I searched and found the stuff. I'm not sure if she was found guilty or not, but I know the court placed her in foster care and she went to the continuation school. A sorta happy ending, I guess.

> *"The reason why kids are crazy is because*
> *nobody can face the responsibility of*
> *bringing them up."*
> *- John Lennon*

Excuse Me! 'My Mom was getting out of jail and I wanted to be there. I was there when she went in.'

151

Aw Nesta Gawd This Really Happened

Fish Rustlin'

"Someone rustled the grand champion fish!!" That's what the mother said and she was not happy. It seems that the grand champion catfish at the county fair disappeared sometime between the auction and the delivery to the buyer. The buyer had coughed up $65 a pound for three catfish that, in my opinion, looked like, well, catfish. Now they were gone.

Her son had over $600 coming and no fish to deliver. There was a security guy, who didn't see much, guarding the fish tank at the fair where the rustling allegedly occurred. Somehow, however, this was my fault. I bought a pig, for god's sake. Why are they mad at me?

Well, it seems that the leading suspect, at least in the mother's mind, was seen near the fish tank by some of the rabbit folks, or maybe the rabbits. No one seemed to be quite sure. He happened to have finished second in the judging, so he had a fishy motive. Some said he was a real sore loser, but he said when the rabbits saw him, he was removing his own fish. Our ag teachers, Mom alleged, were conducting some sort of cover up to protect the suspected rustler. A fishy conspiracy, she charged!! I told her to report it to the police. This was the first meeting.

The ag teachers, in fact, had hustled (not rustled) out to console the buyer, who was an ardent supporter (why else would someone pay $600+ for a few fish?). The buyer, a classy businessman, said something like, "I don't even like fish, give me something that swims to show my kids and I'll pay the money." This was explained at meeting number two.

Stupid me thought everyone would be happy, since there was scant evidence to hang any rustlers. Oh, but there was still the coverup issue, a motive, a bit of evidence and the rabbit witness. Since I was no help, Mom decided to skip the police, confront the suspect and contact the fair manager.

The suspect and his father did not take lightly to the allegations. "Rustlin' is a very serious charge in this county," they said. They felt the ag teachers were believing this crazy lady. Furthermore, the teachers had provided little supervision, so, along with me, were the real bad guys. This was meeting number three.

The fair manager wasn't sure why his security guy didn't smell something fishy, but he was very sure that the teachers and I had screwed something up. I told him, "We do not have the fish and do not know who does." He was not satisfied and threatened to withhold the suspect's money for the fish that he had sold to another buyer. A little frontier justice, I suppose. If it had been a steer, he mighta suggested a lynching. This was meeting number four.

This made the mother a little happier, I think, but did not seem to amuse the suspect and his father. They insisted that the school should pay the money if the fair didn't, since somehow we had been responsible for this whole mess. They were not pleasant and respectful. I said, "We do not have the fish and do not know who does." This was meeting number five.

At meeting number six, the superintendent and I met with the ag teachers and we all agreed that we did not rustle the fish. In fact, we could not even think of anything we did wrong. In fact, by taking care of the buyer and getting the seller his money, we thought we had actually solved the problem, if not the mystery.

Meeting number seven was with the school board, who had already been individually bombarded by all the involved parties, except maybe the fish. The alleged rustler's dad gave a scathing diatribe on how inept the school people were in this fishcapade. He called for the hooking and filleting of most of the school folks. And he's on his way to the fair board.

I just know this is not going to be good enough. There will be more meetings. This fish thing is becoming a full time job. No one is going to be happy, but why are they mad at me? I am not a rustler. I do not have the fish. I don't even like fish . . . . .

The Principal's Creed

There is something I don't know that I'm supposed to know
I don't know what it is I don't know, yet I'm supposed to
    know
And I feel I look stupid if I seem not to know it
    And not know what it is I don't know
Therefore I pretend I know it
This is nerve-wracking
    Since I don't know what I must pretend to know
Therefore I pretend to know nothing.

- Mickey Bitsko

Excuse Me! 'My dog killed our goat and I had to bury the goat.'

What a System

Neil is a senior, quite bright and very good looking. He dresses nicely and can be personable, if not downright charming. In fact, he is quite a talker; some would say an excellent con man. His high school years have been one lie, theft or con game after another. He's talked his way out of jams that would have done in a lesser bullshitter. Neil's good at what he does.

However, this last one takes the cake. I heard it all right here in my office. I swear I'm not making this up. Seems Neil "borrowed" his father's ATM card and made a dozen or so withdrawals to the tune of over two thousand bucks. Although Dad doesn't pay a lot of attention to Neil, he happened to notice this when the bill rolled in.

The money, of course, was long gone. Neil and Dad got into an argument and scuffle when Neil tried to b.s. his way out of this one. No serious blows, just a lot of angry, ugly words and some shoving. Well, old Neil was never one to stand there and take that kind of abuse. Even though Dad swears Neil shoved him first, the boy turned his Dad into Child Protective Services, and they began their child abuse investigation.

In the meantime, Dad discovers that he can't recover the money unless he reports the ATM card stolen and presses charges. So he calls the police. When they talk to Neil, he denies the crime. Dad has witnesses and a case and the six felonies will stick. One little catch - Neil is a minor and entitled to a lawyer and since Dad has a good job, he'll get the bill. And if Neil has a lawyer, Dad will certainly need one for himself.

So here's the deal. Dad can maybe get his money back if he hires two lawyers, convicts the kid and has him become a ward of the court. Now the court will undoubtedly lock the kid up for awhile and then bill Dad for his room and board at juvenile hall. If he's then placed in a foster home, he'll get the bill for that too. He also has to defend himself against the abuse charges.

Can this all be true? Dad swears it is and Neil's not talking to anyone but a lawyer or CPS investigator. Dad is about to go crazy and Neil is about to get off again, because old Dad isn't much able to so anything within the system. Dad is not happy. It wouldn't surprise me if Neil had a bad accident.

> *"Like its politicians and its wars, society*
> *has the teenagers it deserves."*
>
> *- J. B. Priestley*

Excuse Me! 'Melissa was absent because we thought we were moving.'

Principal Thoughts *Bluffer*

Snakes

Snakes have a bad rap. Nearly everyone hates snakes. Many are darn right scared to death of them. Yet if you talk to someone like Mr. Lint, who knows a lot about them, you'll learn some surprising facts. Snakes are a valuable part of the ecosystem. They tend to be rather shy, mind their own business and even the poisonous ones are harmless if left alone.

It seems that snakes could use a good press agent to improve their terrible image. I think the same could be said for teenagers. Like snakes, the few poisonous teens seem to get all the attention. Nearly all the rest are far less harmful than people imagine and most actually are quite good for the ecosystem.

I realize that few people will choose to love rattlesnakes, or harmless gopher snakes, even if they know that they eat a whole bunch of dirty rodents. However, it might be nice if more people took the time to learn the truth about our reptilian friends - and teenagers, for that matter.

We could ask Mr. Lint, but it seems unlikely that snakes give a hoot if anyone likes them or not. That alone separates them from teenagers. The vast majority of the non-poisonous teens feel badly that they are often viewed as vipers. It is not fun being scorned for the acts of a few and having your many positive attributes and contributions overlooked.

Not long ago, I received a call from the owner of a Modesto radio station that sponsored a volleyball tourney. He went on and on about how well behaved our volleyball team was and that our whole community should be proud. We are very proud. This kind of feedback is not an uncommon event. Our students, whether it be FFA, the band or whatever, are consistently complimented.

Yet the same day's paper had a lead article on teen violence, another on teen pregnancy. The rattlers have a press agent, the good guys don't. Sometimes I think it's a conspiracy to keep teens in their place. Whatever it is, I find it sad that there seems to be so much effort seeking bad news. This promotes a lot of unnecessary fear and suspicion.

Several years ago, there was a woman down the street who called me at least once a week. She would hysterically screech, "they're congregating again, they're congregating, I'm calling the police!" I always went down there and sure enough, there were three, four, sometimes five teens standing on the sidewalk talking. I'd tell them to move on and the woman would close the curtain. I don't know what happened to her. A group of six probably scared her to death.

This poor lady was truly frightened of these "congregaters." That may be partly our fault. We need to control litter, drive sanely and respect private property to and from school. We can also do more to get the public, particularly senior citizens, into our school. They would love homecoming, the musical or maybe just a tour of the school. They'd discover that teens are indeed human and, at least at this school, quite friendly and polite. We can be our own positive press agent.

Now this is not to say that even normal teens cannot do a variety of inconsiderate and dumb things. It just seems that more good would result if we spent as much time rewarding good behavior as we do yapping about the minority of pit vipers among us. Red Bluff High has some of the nicest reptiles I've ever met.

Excuse Me! 'It all started when he hit me back . . .'

KATHLEEN A. WHEELER
District Superintendent

JOE PELANCONI
Principal

JANICE BLUNCK
Associate Principal

Red Bluff Union High School

(530) 529-8710
Fax (530) 529-8739
1260 Union Street
P.O. Box 1507
Red Bluff, California 96080

ARMAND BRETT
Associate Principal

BOB BRYSON
Associate Principal

RICK PRESTWOOD
Associate Principal

April 14, 1998

Dear Ms. Evans,

Your continued support of our Italian exchange program is commendable. As you know, your daughter was an active participant, taking full advantage of every new cultural experience that was available. Unfortunately, we were not able to monitor all situations.

Consequently, you may, at some time in the future, discover that your daughter may have certain body parts adorned with the Medici coat of arms or another Italian souvenir. Rest assured, this was not an authorized part of the exchange experience.

Should you find the artwork offensive, the enclosed flyer re: tattoo removal may be of use to you. May I apologize in advance if her torso bears some grotesque marking. I must also regretfully inform you that our insurance does not cover this removal procedure.

Sincerely,

Joe and Sue Pelanconi
Exchange Leaders

Principal Thoughts *Bluffer*

The Gown Search

The Winter Formal and Senior Prom are special events. We have about seven or eight hundred teenagers attend, with half looking like a brigade of black and white penguins. The other half is wearing a stunning assortment of colorful plumage. The smart tuxedos and beautiful gowns tend to make one forget that these are normal teenagers, who usually live in jeans and sweatshirts. An alien could mistake a prom for a presidential inaugural ball.

These events are good things. They are rights of passage. Teenagers don't even chew gum when they get dressed up like this. It's out to dinner, using forks, knives, napkins and all those amenities that are optional at Taco Bell. Parents are proud to have those photos on the mantel with Janie and her date looking clean cut, grown up and civilized.

As the father of two daughters who attended this high school, I know we still have those photos somewhere. However, what I remember best is the search for the gown – and I wasn't even involved, since it's a mother/daughter thing.

A few times the search went well. It was probably a mother/daughter bonding time. Other more memorable searches were a family trauma. There were major discrepancies on how much skin the gown should cover. There were considerations about what everybody else might be wearing, since having the same gown as Hilda could be a disaster of significant proportions. I remember one time when they came home with a dress and still didn't speak to each other for three days.

Then there was the cost. One can spend a lot of money on these things. Fathers understand that it is sometimes wise to buy expensive shoes because they will wear well. They don't understand at all the prom gown law that says you can only wear a prom dress once. I was quick to point out to my daughters that they paid more for a prom dress than I had paid for a car when I was in high school – and I drove the car every day till it died. They were not impressed.

Today I read about a special sale called "Second Time's a Charm" at Mira Loma High School in Sacramento. A group of mothers are reselling formal dresses. Dresses worn only one time and originally costing $200 at Macy's are going for $50. They plan to have over 200 dresses on sale. A father must have thought of this idea. That car I bought was used.

I'd like to see this in Red Bluff. In fact, I'd suggest that fathers run the sale. Why should it just be a mother/daughter bonding experience? I can see Dad now. . . "Janie, don't you just love this pink taffeta lined gown, with silver sequins and poofy sleeves? I think we can get it for forty bucks."

Okay, the father thing is a bit far fetched, but recycling is still a good idea.

Excuse Me! 'Betsy has kind of an odd shape. We had to go to the Bay Area to get her a Prom dress.'

This Is What We Do

Friday Night Football

When I retire, I am going to attend a high school football game. I am going to watch every play, read the program, take in the halftime show, eat a hot dog, all that kind of stuff. I may yell at the officials, maybe the coaches and certainly, the principal, if I see one. I think I'll enjoy it.

I only remember one year where this principal actually watched the games. Our team stunk, the crowds were small, fans left early and the hecklers yelled at the coach. However, as long as I'm a principal and we win, I'll be there, but it's a different ball game for me. Last Friday night we beat Anderson 31 to 28. Everyone said it was a great game. People were in a happy mood when they left the stadium. I know all about it because I read Saturday's paper.

I missed the opening kickoff because I was on the phone finding out why the regular PA announcer was a no show. His wife thought he was at the game. We scored early, but I only heard the crowd roar while unlocking doors for CSF to get ice for their concession stand. On their first possession, we scored again on a blocked punt. Exciting play, they said. I was at the front gate trying to explain to Mrs. Hammer that the league set ticket prices and I was sorry it cost her $26 to get her family into the game. Yes, yes, I did understand and I'd look into a family plan.

I did catch a glimpse of their first touchdown, but missed the second. I was talking to a cop who had gotten a report that someone in our student cheering section was flashing the crowd. A few older fans were a bit fired up. A Board Member snagged me and took the kickoff and two first downs to tell me he heard our tailback was on drugs.

The first half ended with several turnovers, one an exciting interception at the goal line. I didn't see them, since I was looking for an Anderson administrator and asking him to help us keep the junior high kids on his side in the stands. We didn't need another lawsuit. The half ended with us agreeing that 7th and 8th graders should be banned from games unless sedated and sitting with their parents.

Folks said the band looked good at halftime. I was with crying Ryan. We were waiting for his mother to come and pick him up. Seems the cop had fingered the flasher. Ryan had a fake penis that he put between his legs, standing up to the glee of schoolmates and horror of everyone else. Ryan was wailing that he didn't see any old people and he'd apologize to them if I didn't tell his mother.

The second half was very exciting. I didn't see much of it. An Anderson kid was hurt, looked like a broken leg. I went over, made sure the ambulance got out of the parking lot. I did see two kids and some empty beer cans near a pickup truck in the parking lot, but pretended they were invisible and headed back to see the game. The crowd had been going crazy. I heard the late PA guy say it was tied 21 all.

I got back in time to deal with two jerks who were throwing dog biscuits at the cheerleaders. I'm sure it involved more, but these two admitted had they been tossing the milk bones and I wasn't in an investigative mode. I escorted them out of the game and promised to have the VP meet them Monday morning. Heading back, two girls stopped me to report that a toilet in the girls' restroom was over flowing. I found a custodian and sent her in there. I guess she fixed it.

With the cash box under my arm, I watched the end of the game. It ended with a 45 yard field goal and a great win for us. Everyone on our side went home happy. I went home tired. I'm getting too old to not enjoy going to football games. We have a lot of seniors on the team.   Maybe next year we'll be lousy. Maybe I'll retire.

"All ballplayers should quit when it starts to feel as if all the baselines run uphill."

- Babe Ruth

Excuse Me! 'He has terminal senioritus.'

September 1, 2001

Dear Dr. (Almost) Wheeler:

Woody Allen once said that 85% of life is just showing up. With those words in mind, I am proud to note that I have showed up for my work life at Salisbury and Red Bluff High Schools for 31 years. For me, it has been a wonderful experience that will end on December 31, 2001. It is on that date that I plan to retire, resigning my position as an employee of Red Bluff Joint Union High School District.

I am grateful for having had the opportunity to work with such talented colleagues and competent school boards, who were consistently supportive as well as tolerant of my quirks. The past few years, with you, Dr. (Almost) Wheeler, have been particularly enjoyable and memorable.

Our District has a great school system and anyone familiar with education and thinking differently is absolutely clueless. It has been a unique situation and I would not change any part of it. I will leave convinced that the young people of our community are absolutely special and that I was privileged to have spent 31 years showing up and being with them. I learned so much. Thank you.

Sincerely,

Joe Pelanconi

Good-byes from the Heart

Well, dude, I heard you are retiring. I got this wonderful assignment in my keyboarding class to write you a letter, so here it is.

I am sad you're leaving, but don't exactly know you. I haven't had the luxury of being in your office, which my mother says is a good thing.

This school will not be the same without you, but it will feel the same to us.

I hope you have a good time not doing anything. Maybe you can go back to Italy.

I am only a freshman and don't know much, but you must have been a good principal. I haven't heard anything bad and you always find out the bad stuff first.

It's better to retire than to just one day kick the bucket while you are trying to do your job.

What are you going to do? Are you going to get involved in things around town or stay cooped up in your house all day long and never come out?

You will be missed, but I have one question. Who will be your predecessor?

I have some advice for you. When my grandpa retired he traveled to Yellowstone Park in his motor home with my grandma. He said that was cool.

I think it is a good deal that you get to stay home and do nothing all day long and still get a check in the mail.

My grandpa and grandma are retired and they go to yard sales all the time to keep busy.

If you need an idea of what to do in retirement, the Boardwalk at Santa Cruz is really cool.

Thank you for all the headaches you have gone through just to make us stand out from other schools.

The principal job must be like the Army 'It's the hardest job you'll ever love.'

"How did it get so late so soon?"
- Dr. Seuss

PWJ PUBLISHING TITLES
POETRY BY PATRICIA WELLINGHAM-JONES

Don't Turn Away: Poems About Breast Cancer
> Reflections of a survivor. Pushcart prize nominee
> ISBN 0-939221-16-0
> 22 pages, saddle stitch, 2000
> $5

Labyrinth: Poems & Prose
> 33 writers on the ancient symbol of life's passage and spiritual pilgrimage, the labyrinth.
> ISBN 0-939221-18-7
> 82 pages, perfect bound, 2001
> photos and drawings
> $12.50

River Voices: Poets of Butte, Shasta, Tehama and Trinity Counties, California
> with Nancy S. Culbertson
> 28 poets from four counties as the upper end of the great Sacramento River Valley in north central California speak of many things.
> ISBN 0-939221-13-6
> 98 pages, perfect bound, 1997
> $12.50

Big Day on the Ranch and other Light Verse
> Poems about rural California
> ISBN 0-939221-14-4
> 32 pages, spiral bound, 1997
> $5

Our Seventeen Years
> Poems of a life together.
> ISBN 0-939221-11-X
> 28 pages, saddle stitch, 1996
> $5

PWJ Publishing
PO BOX 238, Tehama, CA 96090-0238
e-mail pwj@tco.net